THE REFLECTIVE SUPERVISOR:
A PRACTICAL GUIDE FOR EDUCATORS

Raymond L. Calabrese
Sally J. Zepeda

EYE ON EDUCATION
6 DEPOT WAY WEST, SUITE 106
LARCHMONT, NY 10538
(914) 833-0551
(914) 833-0761 fax

ISBN 1-883001-38-2

Library of Congress Cataloging-in-Publication Data

```
Calabrese, Raymond L., 1942-
    The reflective supervisor : a practical guide for educators / by
Ray Calabrese and Sally Zepeda.
      p.   cm.
    Includes bibliographical references.
    ISBN 1-883001-38-2
    1. School supervision--United States.  2. School supervisors-
-United States.   I. Zepeda, Sally J., 1956-   .  II. Title.
LB2806.4.C35   1997
371.2'03--dc21                                        97-3483
                                                         CIP
```

10 9 8 7 6 5 4 3 2 1

Editorial and production services provided by Richard H. Adin Freelance
Editorial Services, 9 Orchard Drive, Gardiner, NY 12525 (914-883-5884)

Organizational Oversight:
Planning and Scheduling for Effectiveness
by David A. Erlandson, Peggy L. Stark, and
Sharon M. Ward

Motivating Others
by David P. Thompson

Interpersonal Sensitivity
by John R. Hoyle and Harrison M. Crenshaw

Oral and Nonverbal Expression
by Ivan Muse

The Administrator's Guide to
School–Community Relations
by George E. Pawlas

Leadership:
A Relevant a Realistic Role for Principals
by Gary Crow, Joseph Matthews, and
Lloyd McCleary

TABLE OF CONTENTS

ABOUT THE AUTHORS

Dr. Ray Calabrese, a former public school teacher, counselor, assistant principal, middle school principal, and high school principal, is currently Professor of Educational Leadership at the University of Texas at San Antonio. Dr. Calabrese has written numerous articles in such journals as the *NASSP Bulletin, The High School Journal, Peabody Journal of Education*, and the *Journal of School Leadership*.

Dr. Sally J. Zepeda has served as a high school teacher, department chair, and assistant principal at both the middle and high school level. Currently, she is an Assistant Professor in the Department of Educational Leadership and Policy at the University of Oklahoma.

INTRODUCTION

Supervision implies a moral and professional responsibility. The person who chooses to become a supervisor puts aside personal interests for the interest of the group. In forsaking personal interests, the supervisor is concerned with linking the facilitation of human growth to that of achieving organizational goals. The tasks of the supervisor are varied. They may be more complex than those of the head of an organization in that the supervisor is frequently caught in the middle of conflicting demands of superordinate and subordinates. The effective supervisor mediates these conflicts and is able to make his or her unit increasingly productive while maintaining a strong sense of human compassion for the members of the unit.

When we began writing this book, we asked ourselves, Why is another book about supervision important? How can this book be different? And, more importantly, can this book make a difference? Many books deal with supervision. We are not trying to compete with those books. Instead, we complement them with this book that makes the critical link to practice. We developed a book that is real to the supervisor. It is a book that the supervisor will refer to whenever he or she has a supervisory problem. It also is a book driven by a set of core beliefs about supervision. We believe that the supervisor is a person of integrity. Without integrity, a person may have the role of supervisor, but they lack the respect and trust that is due the position. We believe that supervisors must see themselves as representatives of the aspirations and needs of the people in their unit. We believe that the supervisor is responsible to the organization for facilitating the achievement of organizational goals without compromising the human dignity of the members of the unit. We also believe that the supervisor is driven by a sense of duty to perform the tasks associated with his or her role with the upmost competence. This book is driven by these values, values that are at the core of every successful organization in the twenty-first century.

The value-driven supervisor makes organizations different. The value-driven supervisor makes a meaningful, human contribution to the organization. The value-driven supervisor affirms the dignity of work and of the human being. These kinds of supervisors are missing from schools and other organizations. Schools are in desperate need of them. They are not technicians, nor are they intellectuals. They are people concerned about people. They are willing to commit themselves to furthering this end.

This book differs from other books in that it deals with real issues in a diagnostic and prescriptive manner. There is little theory for you to wrestle. There are numerous examples that transport you into the world of supervision. In this sense, you are taken, chapter by chapter, through a process that, if followed, ultimately leads to success. Each chapter presents a set of building blocks that can be relied on to help you succeed. We encourage you to appropriate these building blocks.

Chapter 1, "Successful Base Building for Supervisors," creates the foundation for you. It uses the building blocks of vision, trust, integrity, and inclusion. Without these building blocks as a foundation, we believe that all other applications lack credibility.

Chapter 2, "Successful Scouting and Preparation for the Supervisor," opens the door for the supervisor's impending role. It uses the building blocks of data gathering, personnel, understanding, and play. These building blocks begin the process of creating an environment wherein the supervisor facilitates the work relationships of members of the unit. We use two metaphors in this chapter—scouting and play. The scouting metaphor is used because the supervisor, like the scout, must understand his or her environment before mastering it. Mastery always follows understanding. The greater the depth of understanding, the greater the mastery. The play metaphor is used because people work better when they are at play. Play is liberating in that it allows a sense of creativity, promotes inclusion, and is something each of us learned to do at an early age. The rules of play are successfully applied to work environments. When applied, they promote a significantly different atmosphere than most people currently experience in their organizations.

Chapter 3, "Successful Decision Making for Supervisors," provides an understanding of how good decisions are made. It uses the building blocks of process, style, analysis, and implementation. A supervisor is ultimately judged by the quality of the decisions that are made. Ironically, most texts and courses pay lip service to decision making. We believe it is a critical skill that is transferable from personal to professional life.

Chapter 4, "Succeeding at Change for the Supervisor," shows the reader how to create an environment for constructive change within the organization. It uses the building blocks of promotion, encouragement, risk-taking, and assessment. All supervisors want to see their organizations change. They want to constructively guide this change. Yet, so many supervisors confide that change is seemingly impossible because of the barriers they encounter. We take a positive view. We believe that people want to change. They have to be securely guided through the constructive change process. This process requires patience. It requires faith in oneself and in the members of the organization. And it requires a knowledge of how to manage change.

Chapter 5, "Successful Organizational Strategies for Supervisors," provides the tools to guide an organization. It uses the building blocks of roles, beliefs, values, and motivation. The major difference between the person who works at a task within the organization and the supervisor is in the complexity of the roles. The supervisor is constantly moving from the macro to the micro. This is a never-ending flow. The supervisor does not have a single objective to achieve. The supervisor has multiple objectives to achieve, each with a different time line and each with a different value to the organization and its members. The effective supervisor is able to simultaneously organize his or her work to successfully manage these objectives to completion.

Chapter 6, "Successful Team Building for Supervisors," provides an understanding of how to build effective teams, teams that contribute to the well-being of the organization, as well as of each member. It uses the building blocks of relationships, disrupters, support, and selection. In the twenty-first century, the effective supervisor is a facilitator. As a facilitator, the supervisor is more of a guide than a leader. As organizations become more democratic, their members want a greater voice in decisions. No longer can a supervisor announce what will be done. The effective supervisor facilitates discussion as to what will be done and how it will be done. This implies that the effective supervisor relinquishes control and replaces it with trust in human . This chapter assists you in understanding how to make this process effective for your organization and its members.

Chapter 7, "Successful Instructional Supervision for Supervisors," focuses on teaching effectiveness. It uses the building blocks of effectiveness, models, culture, and ethics. We do not provide a recipe for the supervisor; we do provide a strategy. The strategy recommended is based on collaboration, conversations, and shared experiences. If the supervisor is able to move away from a fixed experience concept of effective teaching to a conversation about effective teaching, we believe both the supervisor and teacher are enriched.

Chapter 8, "Successful Communication and Political Skills for Supervisors," is the capstone chapter. It uses the building blocks of communication, politics, framing, and benchmarking. We believe that the best supervisors are those who communicate effectively. They are the supervisors who understand politics as the art of getting things done. They are able to communicate so that they can manage their unit in a political environment. A strong ethical base underlies the communication and political skills. If the supervisors choose to use communication and political skills unethically, they will find that they pay a personal and professional price to achieve their goals.

This final chapter is the launching pad for the prospective supervisor and a reality check for the current supervisor.

This book is uniquely organized. Each chapter has a series of reflections. The reflections are located throughout the chapter. You are encouraged to stop reading, study the reflection, and provide personal answers. This allows immediate application of the chapter's context to your own experiences. Tips are also embedded in each chapter. The tips are based on the common sense that every effective supervisor applies to their situation. For many of you, the tips are a way of bringing personal insights to a heightened level of awareness. Each chapter focuses on a supervision situation. The supervision situation highlights one person in a specific supervisory role. We use this person throughout the chapter to illustrate various points. The reader is reminded to reflect on the actions of the supervisor and to suggest how you, the reader, would do it differently. At the end of each chapter is *Pulling It Together,* which provides a series of field-based projects, field-based analysis, supervisory decisions, and resources. Use the field-based projects to expand your knowledge of supervision. If you are already a supervisor, use this area to discover ways you can expand your role. The field-based analysis are data driven. If you are a prospective supervisor, use this area to discover the critical data needed for mastering your craft. If you are already a supervisor, use this area to stimulate thinking about ways in which you could use currently available data to benefit your organization. Supervisory decisions provide a series of decisions to be made by each chapter's main character. Many refer to the supervisory situation at the beginning of the chapter. Take time to respond to these problems. Once you decide, ask yourself what are the consequences of your decision. Examine the negative, as well as the positive, consequences. Finally, there is a section called *Resources for Supervisors* which lists books that will be helpful to you.

Each of these sections asks you to become more reflective about supervision, the role of the supervisor, and the personal beliefs you take to the supervisory role. We believe that the reflective supervisor acts with integrity, acts responsibly, earns the respect of subordinates and superordinates alike, and makes a difference. This is why we wrote this book. Our best wishes to you as you pursue your supervisory career.

Raymond L. Calabrese
Sally J. Zepeda

1

SUCCESSFUL BASE BUILDING FOR SUPERVISORS

BUILDING BLOCKS

Vision
Trust
Integrity
Inclusion

INTRODUCTION

This chapter teaches how to build a solid base for success as a supervisor. It focuses on the building blocks of vision, trust, integrity, and inclusion as the essential building blocks to create a successful work unit. We believe that supervision is most effective when the supervisor understands how to work with people. In our experience and study, we have found that the building of people is a process that automatically leads to organizational success. The process of building and nurturing people is complex. Building people is not a matter of rewards, motivational speeches, threats, or appreciative devices. Supervisors who build people move beyond the manipulative tactics that have found such a prominent place in supervisory strategies. These strategies are often based on the notion that the supervisor can manipulate people to perform organizationally demanded tasks. Manipulated employees may perform the demanded tasks, yet their performance is often perfunctory and completed without a sense of personal commitment. The supervisor may have control over the employee's time, but the supervisor has lost the employee's heart. A supervisor who builds people is able to touch the employee's heart. When this happens, tasks become personally relevant, existentially meaningful, and tied to one's self-image. It is at this point that we can say that the supervisor succeeded. As you read this chapter, examine the various concepts presented. Reflect on the actions of the person in the **supervision situation**. Ask yourself if this person used the building blocks to effective supervision and how the building blocks might have been more effectively placed. Constantly ask yourself, "What should the supervisor have done?" and "How should the supervisor have done it differently?"

SUPERVISION SITUATION

Miles Paxton was recently named science department chairperson for Autowa High School. Miles has been a teacher at Autowa for 3 years and recently earned his Master's degree from the neighboring university. The department comprises seven members. Miles is by far the youngest. The previous department chairperson resigned as chair but remains as a chemistry teacher in the department.

The principal always thought that Miles had a creative and enthusiastic spirit. It was this energy that Miles exhibited in his work that brought him to the principal's attention. The principal had long thought that the science department was too traditional in its approach to teaching science. For example, the department comprises six men and one woman. The female teacher teaches only introductory classes. As a result, the principal reasoned, females are discouraged from taking rigorous science classes in their junior and senior years. The principal had the numbers to prove his argument. However, the principal felt that the former chair was too powerful to challenge. Now, with the appointment of Miles Paxton, changes could take place. Miles was somewhat aware of the issues. He wanted to please the principal. His first action as department chair was to inform all members that the teaching schedule for the coming year would be changed. He was going to give the advanced chemistry class to Judy Carlson.

REFLECTION

Did Miles respond properly to the principal's challenge? What consequences do you predict will result from Miles' decision? What other alternatives are available to Miles?

Miles Paxton moved too rapidly. He made a decision that had long-term ramifications for his leadership ability, his relationships with his coworkers, the programs that his department delivered to students, and his relationships with the principal. Miles Paxton forgot to understand the context in which he worked. The context had changed for Miles. He was no longer a teacher. He was chair. As a teacher Miles was concerned with the preparation of classes and laboratories, assessing student achievement, student discipline, and other contributions that were expected of all teachers. Miles' responsibilities shifted dramatically when he agreed to become department chairperson.

When you are selected for a supervisory position, there are different sets of expectations held by those you are to supervise and by the principal. It is impossible to meet everyone's expectations. The primary option open to the new supervisor is to understand his or her role, and legitimate expectations from subordinates and superordinates. In this context, the new supervisor needs to determine the answers to these four critical questions: *How do I define this situation? What is required of me? What experiences can help me in this role? What is my vision?* Each of these questions provides valuable answers that will increase your probability for success as supervisor.

CRITICAL QUESTION 1: "HOW DO I DEFINE THIS SITUATION?"

This is not a philosophical question as it asks you to give a realistic appraisal of the role the new supervisor is to play. In our case study, Miles Paxton needs to answer this question. Miles is not the principal, nor is he solely a teacher within his department. Miles is the department chairperson. Miles needs to understand what it means to be a department chairperson within his work site.

SOURCES OF INFORMATION

Miles, before committing to any action, needed to gather information as to what was expected of him in his role as science department chairperson. It was clear that the principal was looking for Miles to play a leadership role in transforming the science department. Yet, there were additional components to the role besides the transforming message Miles received from the principal. The first step is to gather information in an unbiased manner from as many sources as possible.

The primary source of information for Miles is the principal. Miles needs to understand the principal's expectations. There is more than one expectation, so Miles needs to be clear as to all expectations. Miles must be able to prioritize the principal's expectations. It may be that the principal had issues of transformation in his recent memory, but is more concerned with an upcoming visit from the regional accrediting agency. In effect, Miles needs to discover the principal's priorities.

The second source of information is the former chairperson. Miles needs to understand why the chair chose to step down. He needs to understand the existing relationship between the chair and the principal, the chair and other members of the department, and the science chair and other chairs in the school. The former chair may still command significant respect. Alienating the former chair could prevent Miles from successfully leading and managing his department. Initially, Miles needs the former chair to share personal anecdotes and perspectives on the managerial boundaries, traditional tasks, problem solution patterns, and location of critical data files. In addition, Miles needs to gain *perspective information* from the former chair.

Perspective information is that set of information that will provide him with the opinions of others. It must always be viewed as *perspective*. Many supervisors make critical errors by labeling *perspective information* as *essential information*. On one hand, the information is important to know, but it should be placed in context and weighed with all other information. On the other hand, the information contributes to making good decisions.

The third source of information exists in the experiential base of the members of the department. In Miles' case, he is younger than any other member of the department. Age should not intimidate him; however, it may become an issue if the older, more veteran teachers, are not consulted. Each of the teachers in Miles' department has a view of the department. These people are used to the ways of the former chair. They have perceived Miles as a colleague. Miles' initial step is to consult with the members of the department on their views of departmental concerns, needs, and direction. This information will provide Miles with the opportunity to demonstrate the essential leadership skills of listening and problem-solving. Each person's view is critical. Miles must be careful not to be biased by these views. He needs to make sure that he is open to divergent opinions.

There are other sources of critical information. Miles should speak with other chairs. There are a wide range of questions that he can ask: How they perceive their role? How well do they work with the principal? What do they perceive are the principal's priorities? Also, past evaluations of department members, previous budgets, correspondence, administrative memoranda, and minutes of any chairperson's meetings with the principal are all critical sources of data. Effective supervisors gather essential data to understand the context within which their roles will evolve.

REFLECTION

Can you remember a time when you worked for a supervisor who alienated members of your unit? How did you feel?

CRITICAL QUESTION 2: "WHAT IS REQUIRED OF ME?"

Miles should understand his role. What exactly is required as chair? Each person that Miles speaks to will have a different view of Miles' role. By successfully answering this question, Miles sets the course as supervisor. On one hand, if Miles tries to please each person, he will please none. On the other hand, if Miles refuses to listen to anyone, he will alienate everyone. In either case, Miles will not be an effective supervisor or make a meaningful contribution to his organization.

To be an effective supervisor, Miles must be able to work successfully with people. It is with and through people that the supervisor accomplishes the organization's goals. Without people there is no organization, no community, and no need for a supervisor. In this sense, the supervisor's role has changed dramatically over the past quarter-century. In the past, the model supervisor was regressive and operated based on a punitive model. That is, supervisors set themselves up as the source of knowledge, ideas, rewards, and punishments. They made all decisions. They issued all directives. They were universally disliked by their employees and relied totally on the support of their superordinates. This type of supervisor did not believe that employee "affection" was compatible with achievement of results. In an oppressive environment, these people achieved production results. Yet, in their wake, they left a trail of broken human beings. In time, this model gradually moved toward more humane models that invest in the human dignity of each person.

Working with and through employees does not mean that chaos reigns. This is not the kind of supervisor an organization needs, nor is it the kind of supervisor that employees want. Employees desire a supervisor with certain essential characteristics: someone who listens, someone who is fair, someone who is loyal, someone with integrity, someone with an understanding of the role that the employee has to play, and someone he or she can trust.

EFFECTIVE SUPERVISORS LISTEN TO THEIR EMPLOYEES

When we speak of listening, we distinguish between hearing what is said and understanding what is being communicated. An overwrought employee in Miles' department may be complaining about the lack of supplies for the biology lab. However, the real issue may be related to the biology teacher's personal life. Miles needs to listen to this teacher in an attempt to discover the true source of the teacher's anxiety. The effective supervisor listens and is able to help the employee see the relationship of one part of his or her life to all other parts of his or her life.

EFFECTIVE SUPERVISORS ARE FAIR

When we speak of fairness, we speak of the supervisor treating all employees exactly the same. There is no differentiation in treatment because one person is more likable or another has an uninviting personality. The supervisor rises above personal likes and dislikes and transcends the petty politics that infest so many organizations. Miles may find it easier to work with employees who are friendly, supportive, and loyal. However, once named chair, the position demands that he transcend personal likes and dislikes. Fairness is discovered when an employee suggests to colleagues that the supervisor's opinion should be sought because "the supervisor doesn't take sides."

EMPLOYEES NEED AND WANT A SUPERVISOR WHO IS LOYAL

We believe that the supervisor must protect his or her employees and their vested interests. This is not pure provincialism, a circle-the-wagons attitude. It is the attitude of a supervisor who understands human anxiety. It is impossible for the supervisor to provide employees with a sense of complete security. However, when the employees detect that the supervisor is looking out for their best interests, they frequently reciprocate and reward the supervisor's loyalty. Discovering an employee's vested interests is not easy. Miles may discover a world of difference between what an employee expresses as a need and what the need actually is. For example, a teacher in Miles' department may not want to teach biology. The teacher may express his or her need as remaining in Earth Science. The real need may be this teacher's anxiety regarding competence. It is this anxiety that Miles must help the teacher overcome if the teacher is to relinquish their vested interest in earth science. Loyalty extends beyond the department throughout the organization. We believe that the effective supervisor does not create divisions of loyalty, but establishes an environment where there is a strong sense of mutuality.

EFFECTIVE SUPERVISORS HAVE INTEGRITY

We believe that integrity is a reflection of the effective supervisor's actions and words. These actions and words are synonymous and synchronized with a desire to always do what is right in any given situation. When the supervisor consistently acts with integrity, all employees recognize the supervisor's effort to be a person of their word. There are no backroom deals or favored employees. There is a sense of honesty, fairness, equity, and justice projected by the supervisor to the unit. By acting with integrity, the supervisor begins to create a culture based on trust and high moral principles. Miles may not always generate a consensus, but he will generate trust if he acts with integrity.

REFLECTION

What is it like to work for supervisors who have lost the trust of their employees?

EFFECTIVE SUPERVISORS ARE ABLE TO UNDERSTAND THE ROLE THAT MUST BE PLAYED BY THEIR EMPLOYEES

There is a difference between intellectually understanding and emotionally knowing the role of the supervisor. It is the latter that is part of the effective supervisor. In the previous case study, Miles Paxton cannot forget what it is like to teach five classes a day with as many as 130 students. Miles needs to remember what it was like to setup a laboratory and not have sufficient supplies. Miles needs to remember what it was like to be inundated with paperwork and have to find time to grade 130 examinations. When employees sense that the supervisor understands what is happening to them, the supervisor can be assured of the employee's support.

EFFECTIVE SUPERVISORS ARE TRUSTWORTHY

When we speak of trust, we speak of a supervisor who never betrays the trust of an employee. (The rare exception occurs when the betrayal of the trust serves to protect others from harm or to report a crime.) Trust and integrity are closely linked. When we speak of trust, we speak of reaching deep into the soul of the supervisor where the supervisor realizes that the evolving relationships that are developed are sacred. It does not mean that the supervisor does not confront injustice or irresponsibility in the employee. It does mean that the supervisor can be trusted to confront such issues in a way that protects the employee's dignity.

CRITICAL QUESTION 3: "WHAT EXPERIENCES CAN HELP ME IN THIS ROLE?"

This critical question speaks to the supervisor's experience. Many people with outstanding potential to be superior supervisors mysteriously fail at their jobs once they are promoted because they don't use their set of experiences as a base for acquiring future experiences. In the case of Miles Paxton, Miles must remember his set of experiences as a science teacher. He must remember the emotions that he had when his students succeeded, how he felt when it was his turn to be evaluated, and how it felt to work all day and prepare for parent conferences in the evening. Remembering allows the supervisor to stay in touch with the reality of the employee's day-to-day work experience.

There is also a different set of experiences that the supervisor must remember. The supervisor needs to remember why they wanted the position. When the supervisor was in the supervised position, the position of supervisor was viewed from a different perspective. That view may have been one that saw the position as one of power, prestige, a stepping stone to a much higher position, or of commitment to people. We strongly endorse a motivation of commitment to people who come together to produce a product.

The supervisor should view employees as contributors. Unsuccessful supervisors often see their employees as the enemy. When this perspective is taken, they create an unhealthy climate for their employees. Therefore, it is in the supervisor's best interest for the employees to be successful. A successful supervisor understands this issue. Employees reject attempts by the supervisor to further the supervisor's success. Their rejection can take the form of outright rebellion, or more subtle forms of passive resistance. Some supervisors, when promoted to higher responsibility, leave a trail of anger, resentment, and bitterness. These types of supervisors may see themselves as successful, but their views are limited to the vision of their egos. Miles may have a grand vision of becoming a principal. However, long before he will become a successful principal, he needs to be a successful chair. His success will be measured by the cumulative successes of each student in the program and each teacher in the department.

We believe that successful supervisors must serve their employees and work to make their employees successful. We are unaware of other options that produce results that build a healthy environment where employees feel good about going to work, want to work with colleagues, and want to develop a strong sense of commitment to each other and to the organization. When this occurs, the supervisor will be seen as successful and the organization is successful. It takes courage to put aside one's personal self-interest for the greater interest of the members of the organization; however, that is what is called for in the successful supervisor.

CRITICAL QUESTION 4: "WHAT IS MY VISION?"

We believe that each supervisor answers this question in a personal, professional, and organizational sense. A supervisor without a sense of vision is like a truck rolling down the highway without a driver. The truck is moving fast, but it is only a matter of time before it is involved in an accident or careens off the highway. Once it is derailed, it is nearly impossible for it to get back on course without major repair.

REFLECTION

Do you have a personal mission or professional mission? To what extent do you allow these mission statements to guide you?

In his book, *The Seven Habits of Highly Successful People*, Stephen Covey suggests that it is important, when developing a sense of vision, to begin with the end in mind. This concept is useful in considering mission or vision. Frequently, supervisors confuse mission and vision. By returning to Miles Paxton, we can demonstrate the difference between the two concepts. Miles Paxton, as the new science department chairperson, needs both a sense of mission and a vision if he is to exercise leadership. His mission is one of department chairperson. It is real, it is immediate. He can touch it and feel it. How he views his mission is of critical importance. Miles may be thinking that his mission is to create a science department where each teacher will want to inspire students to study science. Missions should not be complicated.

Miles Paxton has a simple, achievable mission statement: "I will encourage my teachers to promote science as a career to all students." Each time he makes a decision he can refer back to this mission statement. On the other hand, it is too immediate for him to consider it his vision. Miles needs to construct a vision that will guide him as a person and as supervisor. The mission needs to fit inside the vision. If we apply Covey's suggestion by beginning with the end in mind, Miles needs to leap ahead during a time of reflection and visualize how he would like his career and life to end. He needs to reflect on how he would like to be remembered. He needs to embrace a macro picture and move beyond the walls of the high school he serves. In that context, Miles might have a vision of enabling people to see how much science can improve their lives. Again, it is a simple statement, but it has a sense of passion. It has a sense of commitment. Miles begins to develop a picture in which he sees great progress being made in medicine, nutrition, technology, and biology, and in this context, he visualizes students who were educated by members of his science department as contributing to this great work of progress. That is the difference. The mission is immediate; the vision, although clearly seen, is always allusive. A supervisor without a vision cannot have an effective mission. A supervisor with a vision and no mission will accomplish little. The supervisor will be labeled a dreamer who doesn't know how to implement ideas. In essence, we speak of action and ideas. They are integrated and personal, and they serve the best interests of those whom the supervisor serves.

HOW TO SERVE THE BEST INTERESTS OF YOUR CONSTITUENTS AND ORGANIZATION

Miles Paxton must understand who his constituents are before he can address their needs. Constituents exist in vertical and horizontal planes. In Miles' case, he works vertically with superordinates and subordinates. However, there are occasions when he works with subordinates on a horizontal level. His constituents include the teachers in his department. That is obvious. Miles must also work directly with other department chairpersons. They exist on a *horizontal* level. And, Miles must work closely with his supervisor. His direct supervisor may be the building principal, a curriculum coordinator, or an assistant principal. His supervisor exists on a *vertical* level. Miles has a responsibility to serve the best interests of each of the members of these groups.

Failure to understand the vertical and horizontal nature of supervisor relationships hinders the supervisor's ability to serve the needs of the organization. This failure is often seen in competitive actions on the horizontal level. Competitive supervisors believe they have to compete with other supervisors to acquire resources, positions, and so on for the growth of their department. Some supervisors are highly successful at this type of game. However, in the end, it is harmful to the members of the supervisor's unit. They become the objects of jealously and constantly have to be on guard against aggressive acts from other units whose members are trying to reallocate resources. We are not arguing for passive leadership by the supervisor. On the contrary, we are arguing for aggressive leadership where the supervisor always has the best interests of the unit and organization in mind. In this sense, the supervisor helps to build bridges and establish cooperation between units.

When a supervisor builds bridges with colleagues, a cooperative atmosphere develops. In this cooperative atmosphere, the supervisor develops linkages that benefit the unit. In this fashion, the members of the unit are encouraged to work collaboratively with members of other units. Supervisors who operate in this fashion seldom run out of resources and are seen as trusted colleagues.

Another source of failure is the fragmentation of vertical and horizontal groups. When supervisors pit one group against the other, they create a form of internecine warfare. These supervisors spend much of their time building alliances and forming coalitions. This is a form of political intrigue that produces harm. Supervisors who are highly political may gain a personal advantage, but it comes at the expense of the unit. An example of this type of fragmentation occurs if Miles rallies his teachers to confront the principal over a requested reduction in the budget. Miles, as leader of this team, may successfully confront the principal and have a portion of his unit's budget restored. This is a shortsighted victory, because Miles and the members of his unit fail to realize that the money that was restored to his unit has come at the expense of another unit. Thus, a small victory was gained along with new enemies.

There are different contextual forms of constituents: *community, regional, and global*. When we speak of *community constituents*, we mean the community to which the supervisor belongs. These are the people the supervisor relates to on a daily basis. They are the employees who report to the supervisor. They are the members of the organization to whom the supervisor reports. They are the members of the organization with whom the supervisor shares authority. Each of these people is affected by the actions of the supervisor. Each action of the supervisor reverberates throughout the organization. Each constituent within the organization observes each action. Each action is evaluated either consciously or subconsciously. Miles Paxton cannot make decisions in isolation. Each decision, like a pebble thrown in a puddle, sends out ripples to its borders.

REFLECTION

How does your current supervisor relate to members of your organization? How is authority shared or withheld?

The *regional constituents* are the members of the supervisor's greater work community. These people live in the community where the supervisor is employed. They send their children to the school where the supervisor works. They pay taxes to support the supervisor's salary. And they demand to have a voice in the affairs of the school. Each action of the supervisor affects the community. Each student in the school has the potential of interpreting and reporting the impact of actions to the members of the community. Gradually, like a mosaic that is being completed, the students carry the stories into the community and others who interact with the school paint a picture of this school for the community. For example, let's imagine that Miles Paxton, as science department chair, does not insure that there are sufficient supplies for the school's laboratories. Miles will not be directly blamed by the students, but the students will go home and tell their parents of incomplete laboratories, canceled experiments, and discouraged teachers.

Global constituents are members who are directly or indirectly influenced by the supervisor. They may include sales people or faculties at colleges and universities who receive the students who are taught at the supervisor's school. In essence, anyone who is in some way impacted by decisions that are made under the guidance of the supervisor is a global constituent.

Let's assume that Miles Paxton did not recognize the global nature of his constituency. If Miles does not pay attention to the continued evolution of the quality of his science program and allows the program to slip behind the programs in other area high schools, his students will be at a distinct disadvantage when they go to college. Additionally, in highly competitive schools, those students from Miles' school wishing to major in science may not be admitted because of the poor reputation of the science department. One sees the impact of any decision made by the supervisor. It is not static. It is interactive and affects all three groups of constituents to some degree.

Supervisors cannot serve the best interests of their constituents until they recognize their constituents and the impact that they have on their constituencies. Nor can supervisors serve the best interests of their constituencies if they maintain a personal agenda and fail to work with the best interests of the group in mind. Supervisors need to take into account three considerations to serve the best interests of their constituents: The supervisor creates an inclusive sense of *belonging*, the supervisor puts personal energy into the *nurturing and growth* of members of their unit, and the supervisor *embraces differences*.

THE SUPERVISOR MUST CREATE AN INCLUSIVE SENSE OF BELONGING

Psychologists remind us that one great need of human beings is to belong. It is a basic human drive. When we don't feel a sense of belonging, we develop a sense of alienation toward others or toward our social organization. We can relate to how it feels to be ostracized. We may have been a young child in a classroom whom other members belittled and disenfranchised from assuming rightful membership in the group. Although these experiences are part of life, they are painful. Employees who are allowed to feel that they belong are more productive, loyal, and committed to the welfare of the group.

REFLECTION

What can your supervisor do to create a greater sense of belonging for you? Would you be willing to do this if you were in your supervisor's shoes? What are the consequences of this action?

Creating a sense of belonging among employees is a high-energy and critical task for the supervisor. Frequently supervisors make the mistake of regarding group activities as crucial to belonging. Nothing could be further from the truth. Creating a sense of belonging transcends group activities. Group activities that are meaningful are the result of the member's sense of belonging, not its cause. Adapting these **seven steps** assists supervisors in creating a sense of belonging among their employees.

STEP 1: DEVELOP A PERSONAL RELATIONSHIP WITH EACH EMPLOYEE

The effective supervisor develops a personal relationship with each employee. This is a time-consuming task. It means that the supervisor takes time to know the employee as a human being, and not just as an employee. The supervisor learns about the employees, their personal lives, their likes and dislikes, their avocational interests, and their dreams. It also means that the supervisor is willing to share, at the same level, as is requested of the employee. This sharing creates a dialogue. When the supervisor participates in the dialogue and shares personal stories with the employee, all begin to understand each other at a deeper, more human level.

STEP 2: TREAT EACH EMPLOYEE AS A VALUED MEMBER OF THE UNIT

Each person needs to feel validated. When we speak of validation, we mean that each person needs to feel that they are worthwhile and that their presence is essential to the organization. Persons who do not feel valued reduce their sense of attachment to the unit. An effective supervisor is able to discover how each person can contribute to the unit's welfare. Oftentimes, the contribution must be discovered. The employee's real contribution may be far more significant if allowed to grow than if forced into an unfamiliar role. In this way, the effective supervisor discovers the strengths of each of the members and allows those strengths to be put to effective use.

One of the authors recalls taking a position as principal in a middle school where the librarian had stopped participating in school affairs. She was waiting to retire so she could finally do the things she really wanted to do. As the new principal, the author developed a positive relationship with the librarian. Because of this positive relationship, the librarian wrote a grant application to the National Humanities Institute. She had not previously been allowed to write a grant application even though she had requested such permission. Her grant-writing efforts were successful and talk of retirement disappeared. She was given credit for the grant, allowed to administer the grant, and saw herself as a valued member of the school community.

STEP 3: SEEK THE EMPLOYEE'S ADVICE

We begin this step with a warning for the supervisor who wants to successfully create a sense of belonging among the members of their unit. Employees know when they are being patronized. They know when their advice is being sought. They know when they are being manipulated or used. The effective supervisor needs the advice of each employee. Some of this advice may be contradictory to what the supervisor believes, but that doesn't matter. It is not the supervisor's duty to defend a position. It is the supervisor's duty to seek the employee's advice without filtering it through biased filters. The supervisor who rejects advice outright rejects the sender of the message. We all believe what we say is important. The supervisor honors the employee's thoughts, time, and dignity by listening to all views. When this happens, employees realize that what they had to say was valued.

STEP 4: INVOLVE ALL MEMBERS OF THE UNIT IN THE DECISION-MAKING PROCESS WHEREVER POSSIBLE

One important component of belonging is to feel a sense of control over one's destiny. We do not believe that all employees want to be involved in all decisions. We believe that employees want a supervisor who makes decisions on behalf of everyone's interests. However, we also strongly believe that employees want to be consulted before changes are made in their working conditions. This does not mean that the supervisor makes a decision and informs the employee immediately prior to the decision's implementation. It means that the supervisor, sensing the need for change, presents critical data to the employees regarding the need for restructuring working conditions. When this occurs, the employees have an opportunity to discuss the issues, to inform the process, to *work with* the supervisor, and to feel that their opinions and presence are valued.

REFLECTION

Have you ever experienced a time when your supervisor did not consult you on a decision that involved your working conditions? How did you feel? How would you have handled this situation differently?

STEP 5: BE HONEST IN EVERY DEALING WITH YOUR EMPLOYEES

The old adage "honesty is the best policy" is not only true but, for the supervisor, it is the only policy. There are no viable alternatives. In a work unit where the supervisor is honest, employees know where they stand. They know that they can expect the supervisor's words will always ring true. They know that when the supervisor speaks there are no games being played. Employees may not always agree with the "honest" supervisor on every issue, but the "honest" supervisor will gain their respect.

Honesty is more than telling the truth. It is a way of being. It resides in the very character of the supervisor. Employees quickly discover the supervisor who wants to appear to be honest because they are able to read the character of that supervisor. Honesty, as a part of the fabric of the supervisor, means that the supervisor does not try to shade the truth as best as the supervisor understands the truth. Miles Paxton may tell his teachers, "I can tell you this much. There is more that I would like to tell you, but I would be divulging a confidence." It is this kind of statement that lets employees know that this supervisor is a person they can trust. The honest supervisor refuses to manipulate employees. The supervisor is direct and to the point. There is no couching of terms or excusing of inappropriate behavior. However, there is praise in direct proportion to what is deserved. The honest supervisor presents no masks. There is no facade. That is the basis for personal honesty. It is not in always being right. It is more in acknowledging what the supervisor did. It is not lying. It is not in shading the truth. It is not in projecting blame. It is in clearly stating what exists or existed. This sense of honesty compels employees to want to be part of a work unit where they know "where they stand." This concept is simple, yet it is seldom referred to in books on supervision, taught in classes, or demanded within an organization. The supervisor must be honest in every dealing.

REFLECTION

How honest is my current supervisor? Am I willing to be totally honest?

STEP 6: CREATE A CULTURE OF BELONGING THROUGH STORY SHARING

Through the use of story sharing, the supervisor creates a unit culture. It is a culture where members of the unit begin to know and understand each other. It is a culture where members of the unit begin to sense that each person's story is unique yet distinct. We define story sharing as a prescribed time when members of the unit, along with the supervisor, meet and share personal stories of their work and lives in a safe, nonthreatening environment. It is a time when the members of the work unit begin to develop intimacy with each other. The supervisor is the facilitator of the story-sharing group. The facilitator needs to be prepared in advance for each meeting. There are a number of themes that the supervisor can use to facilitate story sharing; for example:

♦ Describe a success that each person experienced while working in their unit.

♦ Describe a frustration that each person experienced while working in their unit.

♦ Characterize a person who has mentored a member on his or her professional journey.

Story sharing breaks down barriers. It builds bonds among members of the unit. It develops an organizational culture. Story sharing acts as a therapeutic activity for unit members by allowing them to share frustrations in a safe environment.

STEP 7: BRINGING YOURSELF TO THE TASK

Supervisors are the catalysts for the working unit. They ignite the energy source of the organization. Supervisors are tireless in their efforts to create a healthy environment for the work unit. Healthy work units do not create themselves. They are the product of intense effort of high-energy people. We believe that the energy that is ignited by the supervisor will develop into a roaring inferno that sustains the work unit. The energy is always present in the work unit, and it often remains present in a dormant state. The supervisor's vision and sense of mission are communicated more by action than by eloquent words. It is communicated through each of the decisions that the supervisor makes, and it is communicated by the supervisor's dedication to duty and responsibility to care for the well-being of the work unit. Miles Paxton carries the match that can ignite the working passions of the members of his department. Each person's ignition point is different. Miles has to search for the unique ignition points. Once he finds them, he brings each member closer to realizing his or her full potential.

SUPERVISORS MUST BE WILLING TO PUT PERSONAL ENERGY INTO THE NURTURING AND GROWTH OF MEMBERS OF THE UNIT

Imagine that it is the middle of winter, the sky is gray, snow lies on the ground, the temperature outside your office is 20°, and the wind chill index is -12°. As you look out your window you see trees without leaves. There are no flowers. It would be absurd to think that flowers existed in this climate. In this stark environment, you put on your winter coat and protect yourself from the harsh winter weather. You venture outside and walk across the street to a greenhouse. The green house is filled with warmth, moisture, and living plants. Flowers are blooming. There are many different types of plants. This setting renews your faith that the winter will soon be over and life will return. Before you leave the greenhouse, you meet the gardener of the greenhouse. It is not long before the two of you sit on a bench and have a lengthy conversation regarding the plants in the greenhouse. You listen intently as the gardener explains to you that there are nearly 500 different species in the greenhouse and each specie has unique needs. The gardener describes the different types of soils, nutrients, water needs, and neighbor needs of each plant.

We believe that the imagery of the greenhouse is precisely the imagery that each supervisor needs toward the members of the unit. The imagery is alive with the tasks of growing and nurturing people to maturity. The imagery is alive with the concept of the vital importance that environment has to play on the psychological well-being of each member of the unit.

This concept is better understood when we discriminate between two activities: the role of the environment and the role of the gardener to nurture the environment and plants.

REFLECTION

How can my supervisor make my current work unit fit the description of the greenhouse?

The supervisor, like the gardener, has to understand the type of environment needed to effectively grow and nurture people. Many supervisors mistakenly believe that there is only one type of environment. These supervisors have a misguided notion that there is a right way and wrong way to do work. In reality, the right way is generally associated with their personal biases and doesn't allow much room for other world views. The gardener in the greenhouse realizes that there is no single type of soil, climate, or nutrient that is effective for all plants. The wise gardener uses a wide array of resources to maintain healthy plants. We believe that supervisors are like gardeners. Supervisors should consider these three major components to creating a healthy environment conducive to human growth:

1. The environment recognizes individual differences.
2. The environment supports each person.
3. The environment acts as natural means to build community.

THE ENVIRONMENT RECOGNIZES INDIVIDUAL DIFFERENCES

Wherever we work, play, live, or visit there is an environment that either adds to or detracts from our well-being. There is no homeostatic environment. One major component of a healthy environment is that it takes into account individual differences. As human beings, we are all the same. Yet, within our humanity we are unique. Each of us has different fingerprints, voiceprints, and DNA. Both our chemical and psychological compositions are different. Each of us has had a journey where our nature was subjected to a constant flow of influences that helped determine who we are as a person. As a result, each of us takes a separate set of values to a common environment. There may be similarities in our value systems, likes, and dislikes. In the end, it is the overcoming of the differences that makes a community.

The effective supervisor recognizes the individual differences of each member of the unit. In these differences, there is the foundation of strength for the unit. Without the differences the unit quickly stagnates and wilts. Although there are individual differences, the supervisor must remember the mission of the unit and bring all members together to create a synchronization that allows for the maximum of individual expression while simultaneously directing this expression toward the greater good of the unit.

THE ENVIRONMENT SUPPORTS EACH PERSON

The environment has to support each person. This can only be done when the supervisor takes the time to enter into a relationship with each member of the unit. The supervisor has to become aware of the various motivations that each person brings to the unit. For example, suppose that Miles Paxton discussed the behavior of a science teacher in his school with his principal. This teacher, according to Miles, was headstrong, flamboyant, and egotistical. Miles did not know what to do with him. The principal, also frustrated, suggested that Miles consult with a local university professor. The professor suggested to Miles that he meet with the science teacher and explore the science teacher's interests. A week later, Miles reported that he had met with the science teacher and discovered that the science teacher continues to work outside of the school as a photographer. Miles did not previously know about the teacher's avocation. On his own initiative, Miles suggested to the teacher that the school host a showing of his photographic work. The science teacher was elated. Is the science teacher still headstrong, flamboyant, and egotistical? Probably. However, the science teacher understands that Miles is a supporter, one who appreciates his talent. In this sense, the science teacher is willing to be more of a team player.

REFLECTION

What other options were open to Miles in developing an effective working relationship with this teacher?

At the opposite end of the spectrum from this flamboyant teacher is the introverted teacher. This teacher does not seek attention and would prefer if no one ever entered their workspace. Yet, this person has as much to contribute to the organization as the extrovert. It is Miles' duty to engage the introverted teacher, while simultaneously providing the space needed for privacy. There are many good instruments that can help the supervisor and employees discover aspects to their personality. The *Personality Style Indicator* is one such instrument that provides useful profiles of the basic ways in which employees respond to their environment.

In simpler terms, we refer to the work of Karen Horney[1] and suggest that the supervisor view people as a composite of three different types: *confrontational, toward,* or *avoidance.* Each of us shares characteristics of all three types; yet, we operate with a dominant style. *Confrontational* personalities are those who like to challenge and confront others. These are assertive personalities. They see the world as primarily a hostile place, one which forces them to be on guard. They like to engage for any reason. It is from the engagement that they acquire their energy. They are good people to have with you when your unit challenges external groups. Their liability comes from

---

[1] Karen Horney, *Our Inner Conflicts.* New York: W.W. Norton (1945).

their inability to know when to step back from the engagement and seek dialogue.

Toward personalities are extremely sensitive to the needs of others. It seems as if they walk around with their antennae tuned in to what other people are feeling or thinking. They are excellent at figuring out the mood of a group. They have an intuitive sense as to what will work and what will not work with the group. They are good people to have on your team when you need to get a project approved at different levels or to engender support. They are natural sales people. The downside of this personality is that they continually need people to be collaborating and don't allow the amount of privacy that some members require. They are often busy trying to be "politically correct" to try to protect the feelings of those with whom they work.

Avoidance personalities enjoy the world of ideas and books. They like to collect data through reading, observation, and analysis. They are quiet people who cherish their independence. At a meeting, they are usually very quiet, but will provide valuable information if asked. However, they have a reluctance to share their information with the group until invited. This type of personality is extremely detached. They need prodding to become engaged and put their knowledge to work for the good of the group.

We can now understand the critical nature of the supervisor's knowing each member of their unit. Miles, for example, may have a teacher who has a confrontational personality. Miles may feel constantly challenged by this teacher and begin to view him or her as an enemy. Similarly, the teacher may believe that Miles is weak because he refuses to stand up to the principal. If both were able to understand each other's primary personality with all its strengths and weaknesses, they would have a deeper respect for each other.

REFLECTION

Which personality type is suggestive of your supervisor? What are the benefits of this personality type? Its drawbacks?

THE ENVIRONMENT ACTS AS NATURAL MEANS TO BUILD COMMUNITY

It is the environment that generates the conditions for the building of a sense of community among members of the supervisor's work unit. The supervisor has to ensure that the environment is *safe, inclusive,* and *open.*

A *safe* working unit means that each employee feels safe in a psychological as well as a physical sense. A physically safe environment is free from a physical threat from members within the working unit and others outside the working unit. Without this freedom, employees face high levels of stress and constant burnout. In many schools, teachers no longer are able to teach with this freedom. It is the supervisor's responsibility to continually advocate for the physical safety of their employees.

Although not as blatant, an environment that is not free from psychological fear creates a devastating effect on employees. Psychological fear may come from many quarters. It may come in the face of the threat of losing one's job, or from being "put down" in public. It may come from constant low-level harassment, or from being told to do a job correctly without adequate resources. In any case, psychological anxiety is a product of inner anxiety that produces high levels of stress, low morale, and emotional burnout.

Environments that engender one or both of these types of fears are easily recognized—members seldom group together, they are suspicious of each other's motives, there is constant bickering, and employees are constantly using sick days as "mental health days." The stress within the work unit is so great that members have to break away for peace of mind. On

the other hand, organizations that are physically and psychologically safe are easily recognized. These organizations are
marked by a spirit of cooperation, a desire to work through
issues rather than sweep them under the rug, and a high level
of respect for each person who is a member of the unit. There
is no attacking or backbiting. There are no destructive side
contests to undermine another worker or the supervisor.

An *inclusive* working unit means that everyone in the unit
belongs to the unit. There are no exceptions based on weight,
race, ideas, or values. Each person sees that they have a contribution to make to the unit and that the unit will not be as effective without them. In essence, each member knows they fit.
In an inclusive working unit, each member is willing to check
his or her individuality at the door for the sake of all the other
members of the unit. A unit cannot be inclusive if a member of
the unit believes he or she is better than the other members.
Inclusive communities recognize and appreciate each other's
differences. This sense of inclusion is not so closed that it cannot reach beyond its narrow borders to other units within the
organization or to other people or organizations in the community. Any act that attempts to restrict access to the group
makes it exclusive. An inclusive unit is constantly working to
form connections with each other on an internal basis, and
they are constantly seeking to connect with other units and
organizations. In inclusive units, there is constant movement
to include others in the work of the team.

An *open* working unit means that each employee has equal
access to the supervisor. It means that employees feel that they
can be heard and that what they have to say will be taken seriously. Openness in this sense means access. Supervisors who
are busy and lock themselves in their offices have effectively
hung out a "closed" sign. Employee's workdays are often so
jumbled that they cannot wait to make an appointment. They
need immediate access to the supervisor. Supervisors who
work at being open and creating an open environment in
terms of decision making, give employees a sense of security
that there will be someone to talk with when they have a
problem, and that they can count on being involved in any

discussion that involves their working conditions. Even in our enlightened age of supervisory practice many working units remain closed and create the seeds for dis-ease among employees.

PULLING IT TOGETHER

FIELD BASED PROJECTS

1. Interview three supervisors in your organization. Ask each supervisor to describe
    ◆   their role;
    ◆   the obstacles they faced when they first became a supervisor;
    ◆   how they work with people who have a different vision;
    ◆   their vision for their work unit; and,
    ◆   the psychological rewards they receive from their work.

2. Develop a personal metaphor for the unit you would like to supervise. This metaphor should be replete with a detailed picture, rich in colors and imagery. Relate how this metaphor describes how a work unit will look once you are the supervisor.

3. Reflect on three people with whom you work in terms of personality characteristics. Identify patterns of behavior. Are you aware of the primary way they relate to their environment? If so, attempt to see situations through their eyes. Identify three major issues in your unit and see if you can predict the emotional reaction of these people to these situations. What strategies can you use to work with their reactions and to make these three people part of an effective unit? Can you determine their underlying motivations? What difficulties do you have respecting opinions that may be different from yours?

FIELD BASED ANALYSIS

1. Choose a school to analyze. Analyze the governing structure of the school. Identify the formal positions of leadership. How do the people in leadership positions relate to each other? Identify political power struggles that exist within this school. What are the causes of the struggles? Are some of the supervisors more political than others? What is the impact of the political maneuvering by the supervisors on their units? In your analysis of the school, examine the effectiveness of four separate units. Describe the characteristics of the supervisors of effective units. Describe the characteristics of the supervisors of ineffective units. How does the principal relate to effective and ineffective supervisors?

2. Choose three work units within your school that have official supervisors. Ask each supervisor for his or her vision for their work unit. Once you have a complete description of a supervisor's vision, ask the members of the unit to describe their supervisor's vision. Is there consistency between what the supervisor described and what the members described? If there is a discrepancy, how would you remedy it? How empowering is the supervisor's vision to you? How empowering is the vision to members of the supervisor's work unit? How would you change the vision to make it more meaningful to members of the work unit?

3. Select five members of your school community. Ask each member what characteristics they would like to see in a supervisor. Develop a list of common characteristics. Compare this list to what you feel a supervisor should bring to a work unit. Do you have these characteristics? What characteristics do you feel you lack? How do you plan to remedy this situation?

IF YOU WERE MILES PAXTON...

How would you gain the support of the former department chair?

How would you prevent the former chair from having too much influence?

How would you build a sense of community in your department?

What would be your first task as a new department chair?

How would you deal with a teacher who tries to undermine you?

How would you create an environment for change?

Could you tell a parents' group your vision?

How would you transform the science department without the hope of new blood?

What is the essential information you need to organize your department to be successful?

How would you act with fairness?

How would you build trust?

How would you decide how effective your program is?

Where would you go for help if the former chair challenged you?

How would you build a sense of community among your members?

RESOURCES FOR SUPERVISORS

BOOKS

Covey, S.R. *The Seven Habits of Highly Effective People.* New York: Simon and Schuster (1990).

Wilson Schaef, A. & Fassel, D. *The Addictive Organization.* San Francisco: Harper and Row (1988).

WEB SITE

http://www.aasa.org (Home page of the American Association of School Administrators).

2

SUCCESSFUL SCOUTING AND PREPARATION FOR THE SUPERVISOR

BUILDING BLOCKS

Data Gathering
Personnel
Understanding
Play

INTRODUCTION

Why do some supervisors succeed in their roles and others fail? There are many reasons for success or failure. The reasons are psychological and technical and affected by nature and nurture. One area that can be influenced by the supervisor is the supervisor's ability to understand the organization, its needs, staff, lines of real and perceived authority, hidden expectations, strengths and weaknesses of the players who work with the supervisor, and culturally determined group functions. This is why we designate this chapter *Preparing the Field for Success*. The effective supervisor takes on the attitude of a scout. Scouts go ahead of their group carefully exploring the trail, looking for signs of danger, places of shelter, and areas to settle. Scouts carefully record all they see, report back what was observed, and provide accurate information to those in charge. This information is vital to the organization.

The scout metaphor is appropriate for the supervisor. How can the supervisor enter an organization with a preconceived notion of what is right or wrong? How can a supervisor know the pitfalls without first examining the organization? A supervisor cannot.

REFLECTION

How well do you currently understand your organization's needs, staff, expectations, and culture?

THOSE who block access to all available information limit their chance for success. They hurt many others in their rigid attempts to supervise the unknown. Their failure is a matter of hubris. They fail to admit to themselves and to others that they don't have the answers. They fail to admit that there is much to learn about the organization and about the people in the organization. They are blind to the signs, symbols, and markings that are critical to their unit's survival.

This chapter provides you with the eyes of the scout. It provides a map with which to scout your organization and the people within it. Once you have a map, you can formulate strategies to make your unit successful and contribute to the larger organization's success. As you read this chapter, examine the various concepts that are presented. Reflect on the actions of the person in the **supervision situation**. Ask yourself if this person used the building blocks for effective supervision and how the building blocks mentioned in this chapter may have been more effectively placed. Continue to ask yourself, "What should the supervisor have done?" and "How would I do it differently?"

SUPERVISION SITUATION

Carrie Jones was recently named principal of Jonesboro High School. This is Carrie's first principalship. She has experience as an assistant principal in another district. Carrie has strong instructional supervision skills. The superintendent of schools told her that it was her instructional background that made her an outstanding candidate. In fact, a board member called and congratulated her on this appointment. During their conversation, the board member indicated that they had found the person who would "weed out the deadwood" from Jonesboro High School. Carrie was uneasy with the phone conversation. Carrie was sure of her abilities and vision for the school. Yet, she felt pressure from the school board and central office to improve instruction. Reacting to this pressure, Carrie announced at her first faculty meeting that she was going to emphasize classroom observation. During this meeting, she used overheads and carefully prepared handouts on the preparation of outstanding lesson plans. She reviewed the observation and evaluation process that she would be following.

Carrie was satisfied with the meeting. She felt that she communicated her mission to the faculty and set high expectations for the staff. After the meeting Carrie returned to her office and discussed this strategy with her assistant principals. At the same time, an informal meeting was taking place in the teachers' room between the teachers and the leader of the teachers' union, Tony Cavelli. The teachers were angry and frightened. Tony Cavelli listened to the teachers for more than an hour. Afterwards, he went to Carrie's office and told her he was filing a class action grievance. Carrie was taken aback. In her mind, she had done nothing more than present a carefully crafted agenda to the faculty. The faculty did not have the same impression. They felt Carrie was going to use an evaluation process that was not approved by the teachers' union. Tony walked out of the office. Carrie sat at her desk wondering how to deal with this crisis. The next day the superintendent called Carrie and questioned her judgment in moving so boldly. The superintendent instructed her to "back off" from her aggressive stance toward evaluation.

REFLECTION

How can Carrie regroup from this disastrous start? How would you have handled it differently? How would you regain the superintendent's confidence?

Carrie had walked into quicksand. The quicksand had always existed, but the superintendent and the school board member did not warn her of its existence. Carrie was not purposely led into the quicksand. The district hired her because they believed she could walk around the quicksand and solve their problems. Carrie had assumed that she would be successful by developing and following a plan to implement the superintendent's and school board members' desires. Carrie was naive. She wasn't aware either of the union's potential reaction or of the superintendent's withdrawal of support. Now the union and its members are antagonists. She wonders if the superintendent is a supporter. It does not matter if she wins the grievance. She has already lost the teachers' support. In their eyes, Carrie was a person to be feared, challenged, and not trusted. This treacherous start will be difficult to survive. Carrie failed to scout the unit she was chosen to lead and prepare the field for success prior to committing to a direct course of action. The supervisor needs to maintain a low profile, carefully measuring every word until he or she understands the organization, its people, and their customs. Ruth Benedict said, "No man ever looks at the world with pristine eyes. He sees it edited by a definite set of customs and institutions and ways of thinking. Even in his philosophical probing he cannot go behind these stereotypes; his very concepts of the true and the false will still have reference to his particular traditional customs."[1] We may have the gift of an outstanding intellect and the ability to diagnose problems. However, if we are unable to understand the people with whom we work and the customs ingrained in their culture, we will have difficulty "preparing a field for success." When Carrie understands the need to "prepare the field for success," she will begin to understand the behavior of the faculty.

An organizational analysis is a critical scouting strategy for Carrie. This analysis is a *formal* and *informal* process. The formal process requires the supervisor to gather as much *pertinent* data as possible.

FORMAL DATA

As Carrie collects formal data, she needs to distinguish between formal data that is pertinent to preparing the field for success and data which is not pertinent. Pertinent data are specifically linked to Carrie's success or failure as a supervisor. These data are associated with the history of the unit prior to Carrie's appointment. The unit's history includes:

- ◆ Unit members' records;
- ◆ Policies affecting the unit;

---

[1] Ruth Benedict, *Patterns of Culture*. Boston: Houghton Mifflin (1934), p. 2.

- The unit's directives indicating its traditional ways of acting;
- Binding agreements with other agencies or units; and
- Plans of action, mission statements, and unit goals and objectives.

UNIT MEMBER'S RECORDS

Each unit maintains records of its members. These records may be housed in Carrie's office or in the personnel department at the district office. In a public organization, these records are available under many *open records* or *sunshine laws*. This should also be a quick lesson for you: Whatever Carrie places in a staff member's personnel folder can be viewed by a much larger audience than she intended.

Anything placed in these records is accessible to a wide variety of sources. Carrie can review members' records as a valuable scouting source of information. As Carrie reviews previous evaluations of her staff, she has to remember that these evaluations carry the bias of her predecessor. If she approaches this task openly, the data she collects begin to paint a picture of the staff's strengths and weaknesses. In addition, each file may contain letters of commendation, letters of reprimand, grievances, attachments to evaluations, transcripts, and certificates of awards for outstanding service.

Carrie must be cognizant of her responsibilities when working with personnel folders. One principal was involved in a lawsuit because they kept a "private" personal file on each member of their school. The principal did not intend to be harmful. The principal was only keeping "important pieces of data for further use." This principal had placed notes in the personal files. Word reached the faculty that the principal kept such files. One faculty member demanded to see the file. The principal denied the existence of the file. The faculty member filed a grievance. The grievance was upheld. In the process, the principal "lost" the file, denying its existence. The faculty member then filed a lawsuit claiming the principal had used the material in the lost file to deny the faculty member a promotion. The lawsuit was eventually settled out of court in the faculty member's favor. The principal resigned from the school district a short time later.

When Carrie works with personnel files, she must adhere to district policies. Any evaluative item placed in a personnel folder should be clearly documented and only placed in the file with the knowledge of the person. If Carrie treats each file as a legal document with full public access, she should not encounter difficulty.

REFLECTION

How accessible are the files of public employees in your state? Review your freedom of information act. What is accessible and what is not accessible?

POLICIES AFFECTING THE UNIT

A second source of formal information that enables Carrie to perform her organizational analysis are the policies that affect her school. These policies are formal in the sense that they have been approved by the school board. They are located in the central office and have direct application to all people who work in the school district. Carrie has a responsibility to carry out these policies. She may not agree with all the policies, but she is obligated to implement them. As a supervisor, one of Carrie's primary responsibilities is to steadfastly implement all policies. We make one caveat to this statement: The policies must be morally just. For example, Martin Luther King's decision to hold a sit-in in Birmingham, Alabama, restaurants in the 1960s violated the law but was morally just. However, because you disagree with a policy does not make the policy either unjust or immoral.

Carrie should read the policies as they apply to her and her school. These policies cannot be literally followed. They need to be examined in light of the *intent* of the developers of the policy. Carrie needs to speak to her superordinate regarding the intent of the document. Otherwise, Carrie may become the rigid keeper of the policy book, rather than allowing the policy book to set the parameters.

Carrie needs to determine if semiformal policies are in place. Semiformal policies are associated with the current leadership in the school district. They are personality driven. For example, the school board may have a policy that teachers will be observed a minimum of two times per year. However, Carrie's superintendent may dictate that teachers be observed five times per year. The superintendent's policy needs to be followed. The next superintendent may alter this policy without asking for board sanction. Semiformal policies developed and implemented by superordinates need to be followed as long as they do not contradict formal policies.

REFLECTION

What customs in your organization are semiformal policies? How long have they existed? Would it be difficult to change them?

Carrie needs to determine policies that are a part of the organization's culture. These policies may not have official sanction but are considered *the way we do things*. These customs may guide behaviors more than formal policy. For example, Carrie Jones' predecessor had established an administrative team that met faithfully each Tuesday morning at 9 AM. This team has been in existence for 6 years. The members of the team have not changed during that time. This group's existence is part of the school's administrative culture. Carrie may not want this team, but she will violate the existing custom if she disbands the team without good cause. In effect, Carrie must adapt to this custom if she is to survive. This does not mean that Carrie has to accept the present way of doing things. However, changes must be done incrementally.

INFORMAL DATA

The organization's culture is a valuable source of informal data. It is more difficult to change than formal policies. It is likely that Carrie will adapt to the existing culture at Jonesboro High School. This is essential if Carrie is to survive and lead her organization. Karl Menninger, the famed psychologist, said, "Living beings adjust themselves to their needs, they adapt their needs to their environments, and they derive from the environment satisfaction for their needs."[2] As Carrie determines which policies are customs, she needs to determine the degree of control these customs exert on her staff. Some customs are viewed as oppressive, others as a lifesaving remedy. Carrie needs to identify the attachment the staff has to these customs. If Carrie is cautious, she will make this determination without causing undue anxiety among staff members.

Carrie's efforts to change the instructional supervision process struck at the heart of the customs the teachers cherished. If Carrie understood the anxiety associated with her approach she would have moved more cautiously. From a psychological perspective, when Carrie expunged a long held practice, she alienated her faculty.

THE UNIT'S DIRECTIVES INDICATING ITS TRADITIONAL WAY OF ACTING

Each unit has its own life. This life is recorded in the communications that flow between members and between the supervisor and the members of the unit. These communications and the form that they take represent what is important to the unit. They indicate the degree of formality or informality that

---

[2] Karl A. Menninger, *Human Mind*. New York: Alfred A. Knopf (1971), p. 21.

exists between supervisors and the members of the unit. For example, communications may explain policy, the social needs of the unit, or new local policies that fall within the purview of the supervisor.

Each document describes how the unit communicates. Some groups communicate face-to-face while others communicate in writing. It is our experience that in less trusting environments more information is communicated in writing than with personal contact. Carrie needs to assess the reaction of the unit members to the various forms of communication before selecting a communications model. When one of the authors was a principal, he discovered that his predecessor had communicated punitive statements in writing, whereas there was little, if any, written acknowledgment of the positive contributions of the staff. This was an issue that was easily addressed. In this case, members of the unit did not support the means of communicating within the unit. They wanted a change. As a result, the change was welcomed. On the other hand, unit members resist change if they see it as harmful.

BINDING AGREEMENTS WITH OTHER AGENCIES OR UNITS

Carrie needs to review the binding agreements that her unit has with other agencies. She has to be aware of these agreements and understand their impact on her school in terms of commitment of time and resources. All written agreements are legal documents. Carrie is responsible for insuring that services defined in these documents are provided in an acceptable way to the consumer.

These binding agreements also take the form of memoranda between Carrie and her staff. For example, her predecessor had given a written authorization to a teacher to teach three classes in exchange for being the senior-class advisor. Although this agreement was informal, the weight of the written document gave it added value in terms of future discussions.

REFLECTION

What memoranda can you recall that took the form
of a legal document? Did any memorandum discuss
working conditions and so forth?

Carrie must not make political agreements without the political sanction of her superordinate or the school board.
Agreements made without sanction often backfire. When they
do, the entire organization is liable and Carrie is likely to be
subjected to disciplinary action. Carrie's senior yearbook advisor had made an agreement with a yearbook company that
significantly indebted the school. The yearbook advisor had
acted without Carrie's knowledge. When Carrie discovered the
agreement, she notified the superintendent. The school board
was not able to void the agreement. Carrie was forced to re-
move the teacher as yearbook advisor and place a written reprimand in the teacher's personnel folder. This teacher did not
have the authority to authorize such an action.

To be an effective leader, Carrie must identify the real and
perceived needs of her school. To choose the perceived needs
when there is no alignment with the real needs is catastrophic.
Real supervisory leadership focuses on the unit's real needs
and then motivates the members to address those needs.

IDENTIFYING THE REAL NEEDS OF THE UNIT

Carrie has a narrow window of opportunity to gauge the
real needs of her school. She needs to be detached from this
process. Being detached does not mean being uninvolved.
Rather, it is a state of high involvement where one is not influenced by data until *all* relevant data are collected. Carrie can
use the following three-step process to guide her in identifying
her school's real needs.

STEP 1: TALK TO YOUR STAFF ABOUT THEIR NOTION
OF THE UNIT'S PERCEIVED NEEDS

Each member of the unit will have a different opinion of the unit's needs. Some members will be more forceful than others in presenting their case. Resist influence based on the strength of the member's communication skills. The supervisor's sole task is to listen. One effective means of generating dialogue is to ask *probing questions*. A *probing question* facilitates the member's ability to discern what he or she perceives as a need. Carrie may ask, "Joe, what do you see as the biggest problem we have to face this year?" Her follow-up questions might be, "How has that problem affected what you do?" "Has it had the same effect on other people? Can you give me examples?" "Has anyone tried to address this problem?" Each question Carrie asks leads the member of the unit deeper and deeper into defining the real needs of the unit.

Carrie can conduct these discussions with a wide array of constituents. The openness of her net will lead to a great catch of valuable insights. From this catch, Carrie will begin to see emerging themes. The themes that she discovers may often be obfuscated by hidden patterns of communication. For example, Carrie may hear similar stories from many teachers regarding the numerous memos that the previous principal sent to teachers. The real message may be that the teachers feel the principal should be visible instead of sitting in the office writing memos.

STEP 2: ASK FOR A WRITTEN RESPONSE FROM YOUR UNIT

We discourage the use of needs assessments by supervisors. Many people who work as supervisors are involved in writing or responding to needs assessments. Needs assessments, unless they are carefully constructed, seldom provide critical data for the supervisor. On the other hand, written data is essential. Carrie can request that her staff complete this statement: *"If I were supervisor, I would immediately address these issues...."* Carrie can give her staff instructions to submit information anonymously. When Carrie uses this approach, she provides members with an opportunity to "unload" and not be hurt. The staff does not have to determine Carrie's intent before submitting their comments. This allows Carrie to hear her staff's emotional reactions. The emotional tone will help Carrie determine pressing priorities. Most people have a difficult time suppressing their emotions. These emotions are tied to personal issues that they view as important.

STEP 3: PREPARING TO SHARE NEEDS WITH YOUR GROUP

Carrie should share the data she collects with her staff. The sharing of data insures that list's accuracy and inclusiveness. Here, Carrie can involve her staff in organizing the data. It is important for Carrie to involve all staff members. The greater the involvement, the greater the potential commitment by the staff.

The data that Carrie collects can be organized in a number of patterns. The first pattern is to have the members review the list of issues. Once the list is final, it is refined. The first refinement stage is to determine if the identified needs are real to the staff. This is a critical decision. Many times, members determine needs, develop plans, and implement plans that do not effect the work unit. Their plans were doomed to fail from the start! For example, Carrie's social studies teachers speak of the need to buy updated textbooks. However, the school board refused to authorize funds for the purchase of textbooks for 2 years. All of the anxiety that was stimulated by the discussion does not change the reality. Carrie can direct the social studies teachers to focus on needs that impact programs and day-to-day activities. In the end, people involved in this activity will discover that the majority of identified needs can be addressed. This discovery is empowering.

> **TIP**
>
> Do not waste people's time with committee work that does not impact their lives.

Once the needs are determined, they can be prioritized. Carrie can view the list of needs from four vantage points: *magnitude, gravity, applicability,* and *time constraints. Magnitude* examines the number of people that the issue affects. For example, the *magnitude* of a student deciding to drop out of school is much smaller than the magnitude of a school doing poorly on a state-mandated achievement test. This does not diminish the seriousness of either problem. However, Carrie Jones' survival as principal will depend more on the resolution of the low test scores than on convincing one student to stay in school. (Note: We believe that Carrie Jones should do both, but we are attempting to demonstrate the difference of magnitude of the issue.)

Gravity refers to the seriousness of the issue to the organization. Carrie and her staff can ask themselves, "What will happen to our school if we fail to address this problem?" Suppose that Carrie is attending a counselors' meeting at her school. One counselor reveals that a student has divulged that a group of students has made a suicide pact. The counselor promised the student that he would not divulge the student's name. The gravity of this situation is apparent. The school has an inherent responsibility for the well-being of the children. The impact of not dealing with this issue, whether the threat is real or a cry for help, demands that the issue be given the highest priority. Carrie must act. On the other hand, consider her choice between two candidates for a teaching position. She needs to make the best decision; however, the final decision, even if it is a poor one, will not necessarily prove to be a grave issue. A simple heuristic to use when considering *gravity* is, "To what extent is the unit's survival threatened?"

REFLECTION

Discuss the magnitude of poor hiring practices. Discuss the gravity of not checking the background of coaches.

Applicability refers to the relationship of the issue to Carrie's school. The chair of the music department at Jonesboro High School has little investment in the supply needs of the science program. On the other hand, if vandals destroy the drums for the band, it has direct applicability to the music department. To determine applicability, Carrie needs to define her school's role.

Defining the school's role will enable Carrie to focus on objectives and goals. Unfocused, sporadic efforts will disperse energies and create an ambiguous identity. Role identification gives members a psychological anchor.

Time constraints exert pressure to solve problems. Carrie needs to consider the amount of time embedded in each issue for its resolution. In September, Carrie does not need to be as worried about graduation as about the statewide achievement tests given in October. As the school year evolves, the time constraints regarding graduation become more pronounced. Similarly, if the superintendent wants a report on unspent funds by the end of the day, Carrie needs to respond immediately. There is an immediacy to the demands. Carrying it a step further, if Carrie is notified of a car accident involving students who were on an errand for a teacher, this is even more immediate than the superintendent's request. The defining characteristic is related to the amount of planning time for the event. The lower the planning time the more critical the time constraints.

Carrie can use these four areas to form a grid that will enable her to gather quantitative data regarding pertinent issues. Suppose it is August 12 and Carrie and her team are discussing the following three issues: Issue 1: Opening of school procedures. Issue 2: 10th-grade spring achievement testing. Issue 3:

Consideration of daycare for single mothers in her school. The grid may look something like this:

	Magnitude	Gravity	Appropriateness	Time
Issue 1	4	4	4	4
Issue 2	4	4	4	1
Issue 3	2	2	3	2

Carrie applies a score of 1 to 4, where 1 is the low score and 4 the high score. Clearly, issue 1, the opening of school procedures was the most important issue. Individual members of Carrie's team may disagree as to the ratings. Disagreements create opportunities for discussion, which allows for a more honest rating. It is a juried process.

IMPROVE WORKING RELATIONSHIPS WITH YOUR STAFF

The success of Carrie's school requires that she use the strengths of each staff member. Each member has assets and liabilities. Linking the assets of all members results in the school becoming more effective. Each member has a unique set of filters through which they interpret events. These filters discard useless information and store needed information. Useful information potentially protects vested interests, promotes self-interests, and is stored for potential retrieval. This information is used to guide our response to our environment on a vertical and horizontal axis. Personal programs at work in our subconscious determine how we respond to our environment. If Carrie can identify these programs, she has an opportunity to work more effectively with each member. These underlying programs can be divided into nine types. Each type is present in Carrie's school. These programs can be identified in most people.

SUBCONSCIOUS PROGRAM

PERFECTION PROGRAM

These people want to develop the perfect program, teach the perfect class, raise the perfect child, and get perfect evaluations. They frame their tasks in terms of organization. They know what has to be done. Carrie needs to approach the perfectionist in terms of gaining an idealized point of view.

HELPER PROGRAM

These people want to help everyone who comes into their universe. They think of helping others before they consider helping themselves. They frame their tasks in terms of moving away from themselves toward other people. Carrie needs to approach the helper in terms of discovering ways in which these people can assist other members of the school.

SUCCESS PROGRAM

These people want to succeed in everything they do. They are highly competitive. They frame their tasks to provide a competitive "payoff" that they can identify. Carrie needs to respond to succeeders by giving them opportunities to "show off" their talent in a public environment.

CREATIVE PROGRAM

These people consider themselves to be highly creative. They need a showcase for their creativity. They frame their tasks in terms of indicating how their creativity marks them as different from the rest of the group. Carrie needs to approach creative people by providing opportunities to demonstrate their special talents. They want to be appreciated for their creativity.

DETACHED PROGRAM

These people are natural observers. They are always collecting and gathering data. They tend not to get involved. They frame their tasks in terms of collecting and analyzing data. Carrie needs to approach detachers to find ways to use their penchant for research. She needs to involve them in the discussion because they are natural introverts.

LOYALTY PROGRAM

These people are natural loyalists. They are faithful to the organization and to the group. They will protect the group's best interests. They frame their tasks to defend the interests of the group and organization. Carrie needs to approach loyalists by finding ways to allow them to express their sense of connection to the organization and group. They are stabilizing forces.

RESOURCEFUL PROGRAM

These people are highly innovative. They cannot take too much interference in their work. They have high energy. They frame their tasks in terms of generating new ideas and ways to approach difficult problems. Carrie needs to approach resourceful people by giving them great latitude of expression. These people will give her solutions to difficult problems.

POWER PROGRAM

These people enjoy the challenge of the political environment. They are cause-oriented and defend a just cause regardless of the odds. They frame their tasks in terms of becoming the point person in conflict situations. Carrie needs to approach power people by allowing them opportunities to protect the unprotected and to champion causes.

FACILITATOR PROGRAM

These people create peaceful environments. They have a knack of bringing people together. They frame their tasks in terms of mediation, facilitation, and socialization. Carrie needs to approach facilitators by providing opportunities for them to guide groups through difficult challenges.

MATURITY AND POWER

Each person has multiple programs. However, one program dominates our conscious activity. By observing her staff, Carrie can understand their primary programs. How staff members use their programs depends on their level of maturity. Each member is at a different stage of maturity. Carrie cannot demand maturity. Maturity is the capacity to demonstrate wisdom. It is not necessarily a characteristic of either age or experience. Understanding people is a result of how Carrie perceives her relationship to her staff. This relationship is best observed by the way that Carrie uses power. Dean Brackley suggests that power can be used for good or evil. It is a decision that is made by the person using the power. In that context, there are two types of power—*selfish power* and *shared power*—that are open to Carrie.[3]

We have all experienced *selfish power*. It happens when another attempts to coerce or exploit us for personal benefit. Carrie will be using selfish power when she imposes her solutions on the staff. If Carrie chooses to operate from *selfish power*, the members of her school will be forced to choose between patronization or confrontation. The exercise of selfish power creates antagonistic groups. Even the members who side with Carrie will do so out of fear of what she might do to them rather than as a sign of commitment.

Hopefully, each of you has experienced *shared power*. If Carrie chooses to share power, she is not delegating responsibility. In sharing power, Carrie reaches out to her staff in an exhibition of trust that says, "Walk with me. I need your help. I need the wisdom of your experience. I need to hear your voice. Let's discover ways to grow together, to work through misun-

---

[3] Dean Brackley, *Organize! A Manual for Leaders*. New York: Paulist Press (1990).

derstandings." Using *shared power* is a sign of wisdom on Carrie's part. It is a sign that Carrie trusts people and trusts her intuitive powers to guide her staff toward mutually productive goals.

REFLECTION

How willing are you to take responsibility for decisions? How willing are you to let go of control of important decisions?

In choosing shared power, Carrie has chosen to meet her staff as equals. She, along with her staff, develops an interdependent synergy. She understands that each staff member is different. Not every member is ready to share power. Readiness for shared power is a result of past experiences. These past experiences are dependent on socialization and education. Some of her staff were socialized in environments where they had few opportunities to share power. They have only experienced power in a vertical sense. The invitation to share power can be intimidating. Carrie knows that mature organizations and people have high levels of trust, but that not all people or organizations operate at those levels. Therefore, it is necessary for Carrie to gradually introduce people individually to shared power.

TIP

Sharing power allows individuals to experience the power that is inherent in their persons and positions.

There are strategies to successfully increase the involvement of members in a shared-power environment. Industrial psychologists tell us, based on experiments, that human beings are not able to discern the difference in weights between two objects until the weight of one of the objects is increased by more than 2.8%. This is known as *Just Noticeable Differences,* or JND. JND is a helpful concept for Carrie because it allows her to understand that the learned experience of sharing of power is gradual. Each staff member, depending on readiness, should be increased in gradients of 2.8% or less from the previous activity. In this way, members will not feel any undo stress resulting from the added responsibility that comes with the increased sharing of power. For example, Carrie's staff has a history of rigidity, wherein staff members worked but were not involved in the decision-making process. It would be unfair to the staff for Carrie to assume that they are ready for full participation. They have not learned how to participate, let alone understand the decision-making process. Carrie might introduce her staff to limited forms of participation such as soliciting opinions or by asking for feedback via a needs assessment. We do not have a favorable view of needs assessments. However, the use of a needs assessment is a low-level way to introduce faculty to power sharing. Her goal is to get people involved through the progressive sharing of power.

When members of the work unit learn to share power, they effectively begin to play well with each other. We learn about people by discovering how well they play together or the reasons that they do not play together. For most of us, playing is something we did as children, and somewhere in adolescence we were told to stop playing. We became too big to play. However, unknown to each of us, we kept on playing, only we did not call it play. We called it work. If you observe young people engaged in play, you notice that play is a precursor for work. There are a series of behaviors that children develop to play successfully that are used by adults. There are several play behaviors that Carrie needs to identify.

REFLECTION

How well does your work unit play together? How is play organized in your work unit?

Play Behaviors

♦ The factions that are represented by those who are at play.
♦ The number of players actually in the game and the number of potential players who sit on the bench.
♦ The organization of the play activities.
♦ The relationships among and between those who are playing and those who are not playing.
♦ The view players have of the group.

The Factions That Are Represented by Those Who Are at Play

Each work unit comprises a special interest group. These groups represent a focal point for internal interests. For example, the English department at Carrie's school has three teachers who strongly endorse a flexible series of electives, while two members prefer a rigid set of courses. These are special interest groups that advocate for their position. They exist because Carrie has framed issues in terms of wins and losses. If the members of Carrie's English department did not have to worry about losing, there would not be a need to divide into special interest groups. Special interest groups are formed as a result of an anxiety-driven mentality.

> **Tip**
>
> Do not allow yourself to take sides or build dangerous alliances with special interest groups.

Carrie may see herself in a political role and form alliances as a means of accomplishing her goals. The formation of alliances creates few friends and many enemies. In the school setting, the issues raised are transient enough that an ally one week may be an opponent next week. Carrie has to respect the opinions of all groups and resist participating in divisive arguments. Her function is to promote harmonious play. That may mean teaching her staff how to play with each other.

THE NUMBER OF PLAYERS ACTUALLY IN THE GAME AND THE NUMBER WHO SIT ON THE BENCH

If we transport ourselves to the playground, we can see some players sitting on the sidelines watching the activity of other children. We will see others who are actively engaged in play. Perhaps you can identify with one of these roles. Oftentimes, those on the sidelines do so because no one has invited them to play. The same rules apply to adults. Carrie has to discern active players from inactive players. Active players constantly try to control the outcome of the activity. Those on the sidelines may be disinterested in working with the group or alienated from the group.

It is not easy to determine the reasons for the actions of the players. The reasons are often hidden. The way we play is not always apparent to the player, but those watching the action can observe it. The way we play, when presented to us by an observer, is frequently denied. As a result, Carrie will be wise not to identify dysfunctional play behaviors. She is better off trying to understand why they do what they do. Once she understands she can alter their behavior patterns into positive models.

TIP

Understand present behavior so you can predict future behavior.

THE ORGANIZATION OF THE PLAY ACTIVITIES

When we observe children playing, we observe a complex set of organizational principles. Children make their own rules, set roles for each player, and evolve new rules spontaneously as the game progresses. If some children feel that the rules are unfair, they either challenge the existing rules and force a modification of the rules, conform to the existing set of rules, or go home. These are the behaviors that Carrie will observe among her staff. Through *scouting*, Carrie will understand how her staff is organized. She will discover a hierarchy of power, rules of work, rules that govern interaction, and the roles that each member plays. Carrie, by observing the play, will gain valuable insight into her school. As Carrie considers her members' play she will observe traditionally evolved rules and roles that contribute to various dysfunctional group behaviors.

REFLECTION

Is your work unit functional or dysfunctional? What type of synergy exists between your group and the larger organization?

FUNCTIONAL GROUP CHARACTERISTICS

It is easy to distinguish the difference between *functional* and *dysfunctional* groups. Members work together harmoniously. Although there are differences among members of a functional group, they try to understand the motivations behind the differences and arrive at common ground. Members consider the needs of the group before the needs of any single member. The mission of the group is of paramount importance. They understand their mission and are committed to its achievement. Individual needs are important, but they do not take precedence over the mission of the group. Members are considerate of each other. Although the group mission takes precedence, the members are always cognizant of the special needs of individual members. They constantly seek ways to incorporate each member more deeply into the group. Conversely, individual members do not place their special interests ahead of the group. Members see how their unit fits into the organizational patterns. Functional groups insure that their mission and actions are consistent with the mission of the larger unit. In this way, they develop a synergistic relationship with the larger unit and other subunits. This symbolizes the relationships that members form with each other.

In functional groups, members work as a cohesive unit. They strive for a consensus. However, they realize that consensus is not always possible. In those cases where it is not possible, they operate democratically. This is not difficult because members trust each other. They are able to keep disagreements in perspective and move forward.

Members are civil and display respect toward each other. Members of functional groups understand the value of civility. They know how to interact. They treat each other with respect and dignity. They respect differing opinions. The language used toward each other is affirming and uplifting. Rancor and discord are left out of discussions. A person's opinions are not related to the dignity of the person. Members see the good that each person brings to the unit. They affirm this good and find ways to allow this good to be expressed.

DYSFUNCTIONAL GROUP CHARACTERISTICS

Members have a combatant mentality. They are naturally competitive. They challenge each other and other units. Each issue and person is a potential challenge. There is no real discussion since all discussion is framed in terms of wins and losses. The need to win is more of a power issue than a moral issue. Although they are more likely to frame issues morally, they are after control. Members are constantly at odds. It is not uncommon to find members not speaking with each other. They take each other seriously. They use the supervisor as a referee. Strong supervisors are challenged because the group cannot accept limitations. Weak supervisors are trodden on. Each meeting has the potential for an explosion. Members walk quietly around each other, measure words carefully, and prepare themselves for attack.

In dysfunctional groups, there is a siege mentality. When members of dysfunctional groups are not fighting, they are preparing themselves to fight with external subunits or with the organization. It is as if they have a paranoid existence where they believe that everyone is out to injure them. If there is not an apparent enemy, they create an enemy. This created enemy takes nearly all of their energy as they discuss, plot, and implement strategies to defeat the foe. A high number of grievances and challenges to external authority emerges from these groups.

Alliances within these groups are continually formed and changed. Dysfunctional groups have the phenomenon of forming alliances. These alliances originate in clandestine attempts to protect self. Frequently, these alliances are formed before formal presentation of positions. In this way, members of dysfunctional groups "count votes" to insure their agenda is quickly approved with minimal debate. This surprise attack is a common characteristic.

Members show little civility and respect toward each other. The discourse between members of dysfunctional groups shows little regard for civility or respect. Meetings frequently are zones where hollering, interruptions, and the use of vulgar language are common place. There is no attempt at discussion since the real motivation is dominance. Dominance is determined by who can holler the loudest, intimidate, and subject the other members to their personal will. Each meeting causes long-held resentment. Future meetings carry the scars of previous battles that must be avenged.

Members of dysfunctional groups are ego driven, with little regard for group needs. They continually place their projects and perceived reference points ahead of the group. In dysfunctional groups, people are constantly at odds with each other. They are unable to grasp the larger picture of the organization. As a result, there is no consideration of mission, of the larger organization, or of the subunit. Organizational mission statements are irrelevant. In essence, the organization exists to support the needs of the individual members.

THE RELATIONSHIPS AMONG AND BETWEEN THOSE WHO ARE PLAYING

When we see children playing, we see the evolving relationships being developed between the players. Some children are natural leaders, and others are content to be followers. Some children will be with the group, yet are quite content to play by themselves. Some children have a propensity to be bullies and others are submissive. The same is true of the relationships among the members of adult work units. Carrie needs to ascertain the relationships between players, since it is through these relationships that she organizes the school's tasks. For example, it would be futile for Carrie to ask a teacher to head a committee if the teacher does not play well with the other members. On the other hand, Carrie may pick this person to provide the group with individual expertise. In effect, a potentially poor leader may be a great role player.

One of the authors recalls an instance where the principal needed to organize the self-study for the regional accrediting association. The principal selected a person for the steering committee chair who was well-organized, able to persuade people to get tasks done in a timely fashion, and able to help the faculty focus on the task without becoming overwhelmed by the immensity of the project. Organization was a gift this person brought to the group. Although this person was not as sensitive to individual needs as one would have desired, the overwhelming task orientation was more critical at this point.

The innate talents that each staff member brings to Carrie's school have their foundation on the playground. These talents are second nature because of their successful repetitive application over the length of our lives. Because these skills are perfected, we no longer pay attention to them. Carrie must develop an awareness of these talents in each member and encourage their use to promote organizational and individual growth.

REFLECTION

How often has your supervisor asked you to describe your skills? How would you react if your supervisor was sincerely interested in learning more about what you do well?

THE VIEW PLAYERS HAVE OF THE GROUP

When children play, each child has a view of the group. They look at the group to determine if the group is a place where they can have fun, form relationships, and enjoy their time together. They also assess if there are any dangers. They determine if the group is cooperative or competitive. They determine where they fit into the group. They determine if there is any cost associated with group membership. And they determine the benefits of becoming a member of the group. If these benefits outweigh the costs of membership, they will not join the group. The same principles apply to adult work units.

Carrie needs to determine the view the players have of the group. Players bring a different perspective as to their view of the ongoing play in her school. She has to have a clear description of what her school should resemble after she has been its principal for 1 month, 6 months, and a year. Carrie should also request that the staff share with her the specific characteristics that they have observed that support their views. Two types of views will emerge. One is the personal type and the other is a group type. A personal type provides an individual perspective of the play. A group type provides grander themes and cultural patterns that form the group's play. When Carrie merges these two views she will gain a blended picture. This picture gives her an accurate perception of how well her members play with each other. This view is important to Carrie because it is the starting point from which she will either build, change, or maintain the way the staff chooses to play with each other.

If each member of Carrie's school presents a view which conveys high levels of satisfaction, then Carrie is advised to opt to affirm the play of the group. She can frame her leadership perspective to use the strengths of the staff as a launching pad for further organizational development. On the other hand, if her staff plays poorly together, Carrie is advised to focus on a model that brings people together to begin relearning how to play collaboratively.

PULLING IT TOGETHER

FIELD BASED PROJECTS

1. Spend an afternoon on the playground watching children play. Observe how they organize their play. Note which children play successfully and which children play dysfunctionally. Identify the behavior patterns of both groups. How would you coach the dysfunctional children to play successfully? What could the play of the successful group teach the unsuccessful group? Can the adults you work with learn anything from your afternoon on the playground?

2. Identify the personality programs that seem to dominate the members of your organization. As you identify these programs, list at least three specific examples that demonstrate your analysis. Once you have identified these programs, ask another member of your work unit about the perception of the rest of the members of your unit. Did his or her perception match yours? How have these programs contributed to your organization's success? How have these programs added to your organization's dysfunctional behavior? For each of these programs, which suggested strategies was used? Adapt a strategy for a member and determine how successful you have been in gaining the member's cooperation.

3. Identify your work unit's formal and informal policies. How are formal policies established or changed? How do

your colleagues feel about the process for establishing or changing policy? Inquire as to how aware your colleagues are to your organization's policy. Which policies would they change? Which policies would they retain? Ask the same questions regarding the informal policies. Which of the informal policies has taken on a cultural identity?

FIELD BASED ANALYSIS

1. Identify your organization's policy that applies to personnel folders. Examine your personnel folder. How closely does your organization conform to its policy? Speak to supervisors throughout your organization. Inquire as to whether or not they maintain an informal file on the members of their units. Are their actions consistent with your organization's policy?

2. Collect the memorandums and letters that the supervisor of your organization has written for the past year (those that they are willing to share). Analyze this material to discover consistent themes, problems, and messages that the supervisor has shared with the organization's constituents. Once you have completed your analysis, ask the supervisor if they have formally attempted to communicate themes, problems, or messages through their correspondence. Share your data with your supervisor and discuss your findings.

3. Conduct a series of informal discussions with the members of your work unit. How willing are these members to commit themselves to working more time if they could share in the decision-making authority of the unit's supervisor? How do these members feel about sharing power? What are their concerns? How do they feel power is shared in the unit as currently constituted? What would they recommend to include more members in the shared power circle?

4. Conduct a needs assessment to gather data related to the staff's perception of the problems that exist in your work unit. Once you have collected your data, pull together a

team to rate the problems as to their magnitude, gravity, appropriateness, and time. Use the jury process. Discuss each rating before making a final decision. How do your ratings relate to how the unit's leadership views the issues? Share your findings with your supervisor. Does your supervisor agree? Disagree? Why?

IF YOU WERE CARRIE JONES...

How would you respond to the board member who put pressure on you to "clean house"?

How would you respond to the superintendent's pressure to increase evaluation pressure?

How would you handle the first faculty meeting?

How would you handle the situation regarding the grievance that has been filed?

How would you regain faculty trust?

What would you do if you found that your predecessor had a forbidden "informal" file?

How would you go about determining the effectiveness or ineffectiveness of informal policies?

How would you make instructional supervision the heart of your mission without alienating your staff?

What role would you give to the previous principal (assuming that the principal is retired in the community)?

How would you handle two teachers of the English department who do not want to play with each other?

How would you work with a perfectionist who has become cynical about the school's willingness to "do anything right"?

How would you mold your "play behavior" to adapt it to that of the various members of your staff?

How would you organize the beginning of school?

What time frame would you give yourself to satisfactorily address the supervisory concerns of the district's leaders?

RESOURCES FOR SUPERVISORS

BOOKS

Dinkmeyer, D. & Losoncy, L. *Skills of Encouragement: Bringing Out the Best in Yourself and Others.* New York: St. Lucie Press (1996).

Roth, W., Ryder, J. & Voehl, F. *Problem Solving for Results.* New York: St. Lucie Press (1996).

WEB SITE

http://www.naesp.org (Home page for the National Association of Elementary School Principals).

3

SUCCESSFUL DECISION MAKING FOR SUPERVISORS

BUILDING BLOCKS

Process
Style
Analysis
Implementation

INTRODUCTION

Each day school supervisors perform one activity they share in common. It is an activity that is inherent in each conversation they have, memo they write, or meeting they attend. It is expected of them by those whom they supervise and by their supervisors. Each day school supervisors are asked to make decisions. They make hundreds of decisions. Research states that school principals make over 400 decisions each day. Most have minimal impact; a few have long-term significance. All decisions contribute to the reshaping of the organization. Decision-making is critically important to the organization's effectiveness and similarly to the supervisor's success. Ironically, decision-making as a strategy is seldom, if ever, taught as a course. Most people learn decision making through trial and error. Those who consistently make better decisions achieve more than those who consistently make poorer decisions do. In supervisory situations, decision making may be discussed, but it is seldom assessed.

Our decision making skills are what we have learned through maturation. In the final analysis, the leadership that each supervisor brings to their work place is determined by the quality of decisions that they make in their supervisory environment. The more consistently high the quality of their decisions, the more effective the organization. Conversely, each of us has witnessed the dramatic impact of poor decisions. We may have been the author or recipient of the consequences of poor decisions. In any event, a poor decision is a cause for regret. When we make personal decisions that we regret, we cannot return to the starting place and remake our decision. The harm is done. All we can do is make a new decision to eliminate the negative consequences that the poor decision created. When a poor decision affects only the decision-maker, the harm is minimal. However, seldom is there a decision that affects one person. Our decisions, whether personal or professional, have a wide impact. For example, the decision of the president of the United States to commit a nation to war impacts the entire planet. In contrast, a Los Angeles teenager's decision to drop out of school impacts the family, future family, and relationships for the rest of their life. These actions express two different decision-making levels. Each reaches far beyond the individual making the decision. The quality of each decision will effect the lives of many people. As a result, we stress the importance of becoming aware of the quality of decisions we are required to make. Each of us has the capacity to make good and poor decisions. The "art" of making poor decisions is not only the province of the uneducated. Poor decision making transcends educational and cultural boundaries. No one is immune to making poor decisions.

Supervisors can improve the consistency of good decision making. They can consistently make decisions that benefit the members of their work unit, the larger organization, their community, and themselves. We are not so naive as to believe that making a good decision is easy. Making a good decision is a formidable task. It takes work, a willingness to cooperate with others, and a desire to set aside traditional biases and filters of information. Good decision making requires that all relevant information be evaluated and applied to generating an effective solution to the problems faced by the supervisor. As you read this chapter, examine the various concepts that are presented. Reflect on the actions of the person in the **supervision situation**. Ask yourself if this person used the building blocks to effective supervision and how the building blocks mentioned in this chapter may have been more effectively placed. Constantly ask yourself, "What should the supervisor have done?" and "How should the supervisor have done it differently?"

SUPERVISION SITUATION

Mark Butterfield is the athletic director for the Marshfield Independent School District. On any given day during the school year, Mark has up to 20 teams playing interscholastic sports. These teams play opponents within and outside their district. Mark is responsible for scheduling games, hiring and evaluating coaches, supervising games, receipts, compliance with state and federal regulations, and budgeting procedures that affect student sport activities within his district. During the school year, Fridays are important days. On Fridays, nearly every seasonal team has a scheduled game. Mark was unaware that Friday, November 1, would be a source of so many problems.

On his way to work, Mark tuned to the local radio station. He heard the station personality announce that there was a possibility for a "sneak winter storm." Mark immediately processed the number of activities that were going to occur that day in the district: four football games and five volleyball games. In addition, the boys' and girls' cross-country teams were scheduled to travel to the capital for the state championships the following day. Mark made a mental note to check the weather periodically. When Mark arrived at school, he no sooner sat down when the phone rang. It was Tom Stilson, the principal of Justin High School, a school in Mark's district. The principal informed Mark that four players on the undefeated Justin team had failed three classes and would be ineligible once the grades were officially reported. The principal told Mark that he could delay the reporting of the grades until Monday and allow the boys to compete against cross-state rival Thurston High School. Mark said he would respond by noon. Mark reviewed the day's schedule of events. He was examining the schedule when the chair of the Justin Booster's Club, Mike O'Malley, walked into his office. Mike O'Malley began his conversation with Mark by stating the importance of the game between Justin and Thurston. He did not want anything to ruin Justin's chances for victory. Mark did not mention his conversation with the Justin school principal, but he intuitively sensed that Mike O'Malley was well aware of the issue.

REFLECTION

What is Mark's more pressing problem? What decisions does he have to make? How would you make these decisions?

This was a tough day. Mark had to make decisions on the renewal of three coaches for the next year, call the compliance committee of the state athletic association, and follow the course of the impending snow storm.

ASSESSING DECISION MAKING

Mark Butterfield is confronted with a series of decisions that will impact many people. Mark's situation differs from other supervisors only in terms of context. Supervisors face situations similar to Mark's each day. The quality of decisions that each supervisor makes has a great impact. Most of the decisions that supervisors make are similar to those faced by Mark Butterfield in that they are presented to the supervisor by the unfolding drama of the supervisor's workday. Each of us can mentally prepare for a crisis. However, we never know when it will happen or how we will react when it does happen.

Consider a few of Mark's decisions. Should Mark give the go ahead to the scheduled games? He has to consider the possibility of the coming snowstorm. At this time, even the weather bureau is unsure of the storm's track and potential impact. Mark has to make a decision based on limited information. How should Mark respond to Tom Stilson, the principal at Justin High School? How should he respond to Mike O'Malley, the president of the Booster's Club? Ethical and political issues face Mark. Mark must remain ethical, yet can he do so without losing the support of the principal and the Booster's Club president? Ethical decisions are easy to make in the classroom. They are more difficult when they have to be made in a political context where professional vulnerability is increased. Mark must make decisions regarding the retention of coaches. He has to consider a number of factors related to his retention decision. If Mark could be sure he would make the right decision in each instance, it would relieve much of his anxiety.

DETERMINE YOUR PREFERRED DECISION-MAKING METHOD

Mark will make better decisions if he is more aware of his preferred way of making decisions. According to some researchers, each of us has a decision-making style. This style tells us how we look at issues, our comfort with involving others, our willingness to search for available information, and our ability to analyze the data that we have gathered. There are multiple decision-making styles. These styles are arranged in a hierarchical pattern. A hierarchical pattern suggests that decision-making styles are not relative. There are some styles that may be more effective than others. In the model proposed by the *Calabrese Decision-Making Style Indicator*, there are four levels: Reactor, Promoter, Director, and Investigator.

These styles impact decision-making methodologies. Decision-making methodologies are a linear process that seldom takes into account the decision-maker's style. Understanding the great variance of decision-making styles among supervisors and members of their work units provides valuable insight into the decision-making process. The hierarchical model explains, in part, faulty decision making. In this model, it is nearly impossible for a reactor (lowest level) to understand how directors or investigators make decisions. The reactor may consider the decision-making process used by the promoter because it is the next higher level. On the other hand, the investigator, a level four style, can appropriate the style that would be most applicable to the context.

The decision-making styles can be applied to the individual and to the culture of the organization. Organizations tend to mimic the decision-making style of their members. As members move on, the style stays. As supervisor, it is helpful to use the following information to determine the organizational decision-making methodology.

There is no one right decision-making strategy. Mark Butterfield has to be aware of the wide variety of situations that he has to face. Each decision has its own context. Mark has to move from one context to another and alter his decision-making style as it is appropriate. The more styles available to Mark, the more likely he will be able to adapt to each context. It is Mark's responsibility to adapt to the context. He has to understand and respond to the context. If Mark applies a single style to all situations, it will result in organizational hardship. Part of Mark's personal training as a supervisor is learning when to make a decision and which style to apply.

LEVEL ONE—THE REACTOR

This is the basic level of decision-making. This is the level we operate at when we have little time to think. Each of us responds as a **reactor** in different decision contexts. However, there are individuals who use this style as their primary mode of making decisions. These are people who act instinctively, often without thinking. They are not afraid to make decisions. They enjoy the energy produced by a crisis. They process little information because they believe that information can get in the way of acting decisively. This decision-making model is appropriate at certain times. It is most useful when there is an emergency and the time to collect information is severely restricted.

TIP

Apply this style when an immediate decision is required.

In an emergency, decisions need to be made immediately. Mark Butterfield is not faced with a decision context that requires this style. Each of his decisions allows him time to collect information. There is no emergency in each of his decision contexts. Mark realizes that he needs to make a decision about the snowstorm. If he waits too long, parents will travel to the games expecting to see their children play. If the weather takes a sudden turn for the worse, Mark will be faced with a level one decision. There may not be much useful information. Mark must rely on the weather bureau for limited information. Action will be required.

REFLECTION

> Can you recall when you were required to be a "Reactor"? What were the circumstances? How did your decision turn out? Do you know any reactors in supervisory positions? If so, how do the members of that work unit respond to the "Reactor"?

Level one decision-makers create problems because solutions are not always apparent. Even if a solution is apparent, there may be other solutions that are more applicable than the solution that emerges. If Mark Butterfield's primary decision-making style is that of a reactor, chances are high that he will make many poor decisions. Mark needs to consider other styles. He needs to be able to gather information and work with other people to generate the solutions needed for this day. The **Reactor** views the gathering of information and collaboration with people as a waste of time. They collaborate only when it is politically expedient.

LEVEL TWO—THE PROMOTER

Level two decision-makers retain the capacity of the level one decision makers to make instant decisions. In addition, they have a significant advantage. Promoters are more willing to work with groups to generate solutions. This type of flexibility allows the promoter to consider different perspectives, generate more alternatives, and consider a team approach to the implementation of the decision. However, because the promoter is closely associated with level one decision-making there is a tendency to adopt the first viable solution that addresses the political needs of the work unit. The promoter operates with a *satisficing strategy.* This strategy limits the extent of the decision-making. As a result, although there is the power of group involvement, there is also the criticism of the group moving so fast that it lacks substance. The promoter makes decisions quickly and adapts them to the political needs of the unit. If Mark Butterfield uses this style exclusively, he will make poor decisions. If Mark met with Tom Stilson and Mike O'Malley regarding the eligibility of the four athletes with low grades, he might feel pressured to agree to delay the reporting of grades until Monday—2 days after the big game.

TIP

Apply this strategy to issues where time is short but the involvement of affected parties is necessary.

When level two decision-makers make mistakes, they take the group with them. It is a case of *group think.* Group think generally occurs when each member of the group quickly settles for a single solution and blocks out pertinent data that indicates there are negative consequences related to the decision. Group think occurs when the decision-making group feels pressured by time constraints to come to a decision. They opt for a satisficing strategy. When opposition to the impending decision is raised by members, they are quickly attacked. This *silencing* procedure sends a quick message to focus on implementing the decision, not on raising objections.

Level two decision-makers do best on issues that are not of grave importance, yet where group involvement is desirable. Promoters need direction. If Mark Butterfield is primarily a promoter, he needs to seek direction from a trusted superordinate. In this way, any tendency to move an advisory group toward a fast solution is in accord with the governing policies of the organization. This also provides Mark with guidance in facilitating the group process.

REFLECTION

Have you ever been involved in a situation where "group think" dominated the process? Were you a "silenced" minority or a vocal, dominating majority? What would you do to eliminate group think from the decision-making process?

LEVEL THREE—THE DIRECTOR

The **Director** has a clearly defined style. The **Director** acts much like a military general. **Directors** do not act arbitrarily, nor do they isolate others from the decision-making process. They make the final decision and risk the rewards or failures of that decision. Level three decision-makers are highly self-confident. They organize people and delegate the tasks of collecting and reporting with appropriate data. The reporting of data is seldom done in a group context, because the **director** does not want to be influenced by the group. **Directors** will not make a decision until they analyze all relevant data. This style can be highly effective. The **director** is able to move organizations, especially if the **director** is charismatic. Often the **director** takes large risks which may lead to isolation and the gradual erosion of unit. However, when **directors** are on target, the gains for the unit are enormous. Because **directors** tend to be isolated, they may lose important insights that others may want to offer.

TIP

Integrate the data you collect to shape your decision.

Mark Butterfield could use this style successfully in two decisions. His decision regarding the weather requires him to quickly gather data. At level three, he can call the highway patrol to check on icing and levels of snowfall in parts of the state where the storm has hit. He can call the weather bureau and talk with a forecaster. He can call the athletic director at the school site where the game is being played to discuss alternatives. By collecting appropriate data from the relevant sources, Mark increases the likelihood that he will make a good decision. Also, those who have a vested interest in Mark's decision will acknowledge that they were consulted.

Mark can use this direct style to manage the situation regarding the four students' eligibility. Mark cannot avoid the decision. He has been made aware of the situation. If he ignores the situation, the students will play. By hoping for a snowstorm he is avoiding the issue. By assuming the role of the **director**, Mark can call the state athletic association that governs high school athletics and ask for clarification on the eligibility rule. Once the rule is clarified, Mark can act decisively. His action will set a standard for the athletes, principals in the district, and booster club members. Mark may not win friends, but he will gain solid respect for his integrity.

REFLECTION

Ethical decisions require decisive action. Recall a time when you participated in or observed this type of action.

LEVEL FOUR—THE INVESTIGATOR

The **Investigator** embodies the positive characteristics of each of the preceding types, being able to function at each of the preceding levels depending on the context. The **Investigator** understands the value of working with people and involving them in the decision-making process. The **Investigator** wants full participation by each member in the decision-making process. The **Investigator** facilitates group discussions that insure the use of an *optimizing* strategy rather than a *satisficing* strategy. As a result, there is an exhaustive search for information. Information is shared to determine the *symptoms*, *causes*, and *sources* of the problem that generates the need for a decision. Group deliberations are intense. The **Investigator** uses safeguards to prevent *group think*. Because of the intensity of the **Investigator's** decision-making process, there is a high level of trust that the right solution will emerge. This type of activity results in good decisions and in the high level investment of the people who participated in the decision making process.

TIP

Set time limits for making a decision with bench marks for collecting and analyzing data.

The **Investigator** can over analyze a potential decision and become so absorbed in the process that a decision is not made. This process can take the group past the critical decision-making point. As a result, the group may arrive at a "great" decision but it will make little difference because the decision came too late to address the organization's need. At these times, the **Investigator** needs to move to level three and be more directive. By providing parameters to his or her investigative team, the **Investigator** prevents organizational paralysis.

The **Investigator** must be astute in forming the decision-making/investigative group. A poorly selected team will make poor decisions. Mark Butterfield needs to understand the issue to be resolved. Once he understands the issue to be resolved, he can bring the most appropriate people together to make the decision in terms of investment in the problem, skills, and commitment to the project.

Mark Butterfield can use this method in resolving the decision regarding the retention of coaches. Mark needs to assemble a decision-making/investigative team that will examine each coach's contribution to the organization. Because a decision-making/investigative team thoroughly collects and analyzes all pertinent data, they will most likely arrive at a solution that is in the best interests of the organization, coaches, and community. Mark leaves no stone unturned, all relevant data is considered, each alternative is evaluated against the same standard, and the consequences of each possible decision are weighed before consensus is considered.

REFLECTION

Recall a time when you were part of a decision-making/investigative team. What was the quality of your group's decision(s)? Does your current work unit employ this model?

DECISION-MAKING PITFALLS

Mark Butterfield needs to be aware of decision-making pitfalls. These pitfalls are not obvious. They are more like holes into which poor decision-makers fall, unaware of the hole's presence, how they fell into the hole, and how to prevent themselves from falling into the same hole again. If Mark examines the following pitfalls, he may be able to prevent himself from cycling through a poor decision-making process.

PITFALL #1: FEAR

Fear can prevent Mark from making the right decision at the right time. There is no such thing as the right decision at the wrong time. Mark is a complex person with a personal set of motivations as to why he acts. Mark's fears are different from those of his colleagues. However, fear is not something embarrassing to Mark. Fear is a natural human reaction. It is this natural reaction that prevents Mark from getting into dangerous situations. Mark has learned to be fearful of driving too fast. He has learned to be fearful of ingesting harmful materials into his body and of walking in dangerous environments. These fear reactions are tied directly to Mark's instinct to survive. They are good instincts. They only hamper Mark when they dominate his thinking and prevent him from taking necessary risks associated with healthy living. A good example is the fear of flying. This fear hinders many people from traveling, accepting new jobs, seeing family, or gaining necessary medical assistance. This fear, or *phobia*, dominates behavior. The only way to overcome many fears is through professional help. Although you may not be afraid of flying or have other overt manifestations of a phobia, fear may be a driving factor in how your decisions are made. If you are competent, there is no reason to fear. You can move ahead firmly in your role as supervisor and know that the work you are doing is being done by someone who is well trained, experienced, and competent. A sense of competence dispels fear and is not related to arrogance. A person is arrogant primarily because of a high fear level. A competent person recognizes his or her strengths and weaknesses. A competent person is able to compensate for weaknesses through the investment in other people. Until we develop a strong sense of competence, fear rules. Fear in decision making is found in four areas: *fear of adventure, fear of the unknown, fear of the risks involved,* and *fear of place.*

Fear of adventure can imprison Mark and keep him from looking into the future. He may see the future as too threatening and without hope. Those who fear adventure throw their hands in the air and say, "What's the use." This type of fear creates a sense of doom in the organization. John Gardner said that above all else, leaders provide hope. A supervisor who has the fear of the future and fear of adventure cannot provide hope to the members of his or her unit. Mark needs to move this fear if he is to be an effective supervisor.

Fear of the unknown can imprison Mark because the future is hidden. All Mark has is the present moment. The past is no longer his. He cannot gain access to the future. Mark can only head into each new day unaware of what that day will bring. This sense of unawareness can create a paralyzing fear in Mark if it prevents him from meeting new people, investing in new approaches, and defining a new vision.

Fear of the risks involved can imprison Mark because of a fear of losing all that he has achieved in terms of power, possessions, or psychological security. Mark Butterfield's decision to not allow the students to play in the game may create a strong political opponent in Mike O'Malley and the possible loss of his job, depending on the power that Mike O'Malley has in the community. There is no risk-free place on this planet. Living is a risk. Each time Mark makes a decision, he is involved in risk-taking behavior.

Fear of place may imprison Mark in place. Mark has grown comfortable in his place and is able to predict what is likely to happen. When Mark is asked to move to a new place he has to learn its dynamics. Human beings like predictability. We like to anticipate what will happen. If we do "a" we want to anticipate "b" will happen. The world of reality tells us differently. "B" may happen most of the time; it is likely that "c," or "d," or "f," may also occur. We term this accident or chance. When we stay in our place, we become set and resist change. It is the natural process for people and organizations to continuously change. It is a pattern of life. If Mark Butterfield sat contentedly in his office ignoring the challenges he faces, then his organization would be harmed, as well as the people who depend on his decisions.

PITFALL #2: INFORMATION OVERLOAD

Information overload is a primary cause of poor decision-making. This is an important factor when Mark considers how he is inundated with information from books, mail, magazines, the Internet, television, and other sources. Research has demonstrated that human beings can process limited amounts of information. That limit is 7±2 pieces of information. Once Mark reaches his maximum amount of information, he will push some information out to allow in other information. It is easy to eliminate critical information and take in irrelevant information. As a result, Mark may make decisions with the inaccurate information, feel a sense of being overwhelmed, or opt for the satisficing solution.

REFLECTION

How many items of information can you balance at any given time? What happens when you feel overloaded with projects?

Mark must be able to make decisions regarding each piece of information. He needs to determine if a piece of information is used in the current issue, useful for future reference, or clutter. Mark can apply this to the number of projects that he can handle at any given time. For example, one of the authors was between flights at the Lambert International Airport in St. Louis and struckup a conversation with another passenger. The other passenger was an amateur juggler on his way to a juggler's convention. The author asked the juggler how many objects he could juggle without letting one fall. Without hesitation, the juggler said seven! The author, aware of the research on information processing, then asked how many objects the best jugglers could maintain in the air at any given time without letting one fall. The juggler replied nine or ten. The author smiled and thought, "seven plus or minus two!"

When the number of projects, events, or problems that confront us exceeds our limitations, then it is impossible to make good decisions. This is one reason why astute supervisors delegate tasks. It is not to get rid of work. They know that they simply cannot make good decisions if they try to do it all.

TIP

Understand your limitations.

PITFALL # 3: PERSONAL FILTERS

Another way in which Mark may make poor decisions may be because of the way he filters information. Mark has been socialized since birth with psychological filters that his parents, teachers, ministers or priests, and others imparted to us. Mark may use these filters to make sense of the world as it surrounds him. These filters help Mark find his way and avoid problems. In many cases, these filters blind Mark to the realities of the world. Even though the objective truth is present, Mark is unable to see the objective truth because his filters block the light from reflecting off that truth. For example, some people are raised in environments where racism is an accepted value. Children born in this environment are not born as racists. Yet, children unknowingly develop a series of filters that continuously dictate the values attached to a racist ideology. As the children get older, they can be presented with objective information regarding the evils of racism and not see the information because their filters are so tightly woven that little, if any, light can break through.

Unless Mark is able to discover his filters, he will be unable to perceive problems accurately, he will be unable to generate the number of alternatives essential to good decision making, and he will be unable to generate accurate objectives that determine the alternative set. Assume that Mark Butterfield has a strong filter regarding competition. Mark is an intense competitor; he loves to win. He takes this competitive edge to the golf course, the racquetball court, and even to simple card games. He is a consummate competitor. When Mark is presented with the information by the principal and Mike O'Malley related to the academic eligibility of the four athletes, he processes this information through a series of filters before he makes his decision. If the winning filter is strong, Mark will suggest to the principal that the grades of the students be officially reported on Monday—after the game! Mark's filter creates an ethical issue without him realizing what is happening. This is one reason why Mark needs people who will disagree with him and present him with data that challenge his filters.

PITFALL # 4: SOCIAL PRESSURE

Mark is affected by social pressure. Social pressure can come directly from the demands of the organization, the external community, family, or other social organizations. Social pressures influence Mark. If he fails to conform to the mean of the group, then they may act to exclude him from membership. For example, in a school where one of the authors was principal, the teachers were in the midst of acrimonious salary negotiation discussions. The teachers decided to *work to rule,* that is, they would perform only those duties explicitly mentioned in their contract. One teacher continued to help students after school and sponsor student activities. This teacher was ostracized by other faculty for failure to conform to their social demands. Teachers would not sit with her in the teacher's lounge, speak to her, or cooperate with her in any endeavor she initiated.

REFLECTION

Have you experienced social pressure at your worksite? How have you responded to this pressure? How did you feel about your response?

Conforming to the mean of the group is appropriate when the group's mean is consistent with good decision making. There are times when the group's mean is contrary to good decision making. Mark has to make a personal decision based on personal integrity. Mark has to decide whether to conform to or challenge the group.

Mark is in a political environment. However, Mark needs to make decisions that are not influenced by politics but by appropriate values. When Mark moves his decision making out of the political arena, he is able to operate freely and distance himself from the pressures of special interest groups and powerful personalities.

When Mark makes a decision that runs counter to the wishes of the group, then he must be prepared for the group's negative reaction. Mark Butterfield's decision to challenge the principal at Justin and Mike O'Malley will create the environment for a negative reaction. Mark must prepare for either party to sabotage his work or career. However, Mark does not have to be ashamed of his actions. His decision will pay off in the long run.

TIP

Use your communication and political skills to educate people as to why you have to make an unpopular decision.

THE DECISION-MAKING RESPONSE

Each of us has a unique response to a decision-making situation. For example, how would Mark respond if he were at a school pep rally and a student yelled "fight!" Would Mark seek assistance? Would Mark look for the fight? Would Mark wait passively for another teacher or supervisor to handle the situation? Or could the word "fight" be part of the context of the rally? "Fight" can be used in different contexts. The word is interpreted based on each person's unique set of personal experiences. The word itself can elicit a feeling of stress, happiness, or laughter. Words awake an emotional reaction. The same is true of problems. Each problem awakens a unique response in Mark. It is a stress-driven response. Mark's recognition of the problem is caused by the *crisis* it generates, the *pressures* he faces, and his gradual *awareness* of the symptoms generated by the problem.

If Mark is able to slow down his thinking and reacting processes, he will understand how and why he makes decisions. Only after Mark is able to understand his decision process will he be able to disrupt his current cognitive decision-making process and replace it with a more effective cognitive decision process. Mark's brain receives unscrambled messages that his mind assesses. Mark's mind takes the incoming messages and runs them through his *attitudes, beliefs,* and *assumptions*. Sometimes his attitudes, beliefs, and assumptions are irrational. When they are irrational, they are the hidden source of poor decision making. Ellis identified a set of 10 **irrational attitudes, beliefs, and assumptions** that can shape our behavior (Fig. 3.1).[1]

When Mark becomes aware of an event, it is filtered through these lenses, which affect his moods and emotions. When this information reaches his moods and emotions, he begins to *frame* images of the event. When *framed*, Mark creates a positive or negative picture of the event. Mark may perceive the event as threatening, challenging, stimulating, rewarding, or neutral. Once Mark develops his frame of thinking, he can apply himself to the problem. If his security is challenged, he may begin to develop strategies to protect himself. If there is the possibility of great reward or success, Mark may begin to plan to take advantage of this opportunity. This set of attitudes, beliefs, and assumptions automatically frames Mark's

---

[1] Dr. Albert Ellis, in H. Benson and E. Stuart, *The Wellness Book.* New York: Firestone (1993), p. 195.

FIGURE 3.1. IRRATIONAL ATTITUDES, BELIEFS, AND ASSUMPTIONS

- ◆ We think it is an absolute necessity for an adult to have love and approval from peers, family, and friends.
- ◆ We think we must be unfailingly competent and almost perfect in all we undertake.
- ◆ We think certain people are evil, wicked, and villainous, and should be punished.
- ◆ We think it is horrible when people and things are not the way we would like them to be.
- ◆ We think external events cause most human misery —people simply react as events trigger their emotions.
- ◆ We think we should feel fear or anxiety about anything that is unknown, uncertain, or potentially dangerous.
- ◆ We think it is easier to avoid than to face life's difficulties and responsibilities.
- ◆ We think we need something other or stronger or greater than ourselves to rely on.
- ◆ We think the past has a lot to do with determining the present.
- ◆ We think happiness can be achieved by inaction, passivity, and endless leisure.

---

thinking and draws a picture of the problem for him. If, for example, Mark has the irrational belief that *he has to be competent in all that he does,* Mark may automatically view criticism of his work as a personal attack. This may cause Mark to attack, subvert, flee, or deny the problems that confront him.

Mark Butterfield may hold the irrational assumption that *it is easier to avoid than to face life's difficulties and responsibilities.* Imagine what will happen now that he has to make a decision to postpone scheduled games. Mark may plod along believing that the snowstorm will go away, and that the games will be played and soon forgotten. This is called *cognitive distortion.*

Mark does not want to assume the responsibility of making a potentially poor decision. However, Mark does not realize that by not making a decision, he is making a decision, and the decision will affect many people.

Cognitive distortions are a cause of poor decisions. Benson and Stuart identify 10 *cognitive distortions*. These distortions are all-or-nothing thinking, overgeneralizations, mind filters, negative focusing, assuming the solution, amplification of the situation, emotional dictation, assumption, labeling, and guilt.[2] When Mark identifies his *cognitive distortions*, he can view data objectively and make better decisions.

REFLECTION

What *cognitive distortions* drive your thinking? How have they impacted your decisions?

MAKING GOOD DECISIONS

One way of understanding how to make good decisions is to understand how we make decisions. When Mark makes a decision he considers a number of *cognitive takeoffs*. The first cognitive takeoff includes *time, expertise,* and *complexity.* If Mark is pressed for time, he will take the first viable solution without searching for other alternatives. Time is an important factor. Research has consistently indicated that the more time involved in the making of the decision, the greater the likelihood that it will be a good decision.

---

[2] H. Benson and E. Stuart, *The Wellness Book.* New York: Firestone (1993), pp. 196–199.

TIP

Journal all decisions for a week and then review the issue, the action, and the consequences, if known.

Time needs to be planned into the decision-making process so that the problem can be properly defined, the data relevant to the problem and proposed alternatives can be collected, and contingency planning can occur. The time expended to make the decision is not passive time. It is active time. During active time there are meetings, discussions, collection of data, establishment of criteria, and the generation of a wide array of alternatives. It is a hectic time.

There may be times when Mark does not have the expertise to solve a problem or to make the required decision. If he feels pressure, he is likely to ignore the fact that he does not have the expertise and makes a decision that he is not qualified to make. Mark Butterfield is not an expert on weather. He needs expert help. If he doesn't seek help and makes the decision based on his expertise, chances increase that he will make a poor decision.

Complexity is another cognitive takeoff. Most issues are complex. They have many aspects that need to be examined before a decision can be made. If Mark believes that the issue is too complex, he may look for simplistic solutions. We are not advocating that Mark take an analytical, left-brained approach and break the problem down into little chunks. We are suggesting Mark look at the problem from a multitude of angles to gain a grasp of the size, movement, and *stuff* of the issues involved. The issue faced by Mark Butterfield regarding the cancellation of games has enormous complexity. There are officials, transportation, the community, students, athletes, parents, and security who have to be notified. There are organizational problems and related emotional issues. The coach of Justin High School may want extra time to prepare, since four stars cannot play, whereas other coaches in the district are ready to proceed. Issues are complex.

REFLECTION

Have you made decisions that you were not qualified to make? How did they turn out? Have your supervisors made decisions in areas where they were not qualified? What were the consequences of those decisions?

Cognitive takeoffs include *prestige, self-interest, and stress.* These cognitive takeoffs are ego related. When we speak of *prestige,* we are talking of an idealized image. If Mark is too closely associated with his idealized image, it will cloud his decision-making. For example, Mark may choose to buy a car simply because of the perceived prestige of owning a specific model of a car. Mark may choose to buy a home in a particular neighborhood strictly because of the prestige that is associated with home ownership in that area. When the idealized image is given a priority, it obfuscates other criteria. Since the issue of prestige is so tightly tied to that of the idealized image, awareness of it is more difficult and it is difficult to control. If Mark Butterfield approaches the principal of Justin High School and challenges his ethical position, Mark may be correct, but he has damaged the principal's ego. The principal's idealized image will not accept Mark's challenge. Mark is better served by guiding the principal by asking a question such as, "What do you think the state athletic association would say if we asked them for permission?" The principal is guided toward the ethical resolution of the situation, an improbable task if the principal's idealized image is harmed.

Self-interest is also related to the idealized image. Self-interest focuses the primary criteria of decision making on the decision-maker's prurient interests. When Mark's interests and the organization's interests coincide, decision satisfaction is likely to occur. However, when the decision presents a conflict over whose interests will be served, a self-serving decision maker will always opt to satisfy the idealized image.

For example, a teacher presented her supervisor with a request to attend a conference in a city nearly 100 miles away. The supervisor looked at the data regarding the conference and told the teacher that the school needed the teacher and that the conference would not be that good. The supervisor used the information given to him by the teacher to register for and attend the conference himself! The supervisor in this case used his self-interest as the primary criterion to satisfy his idealized image. Mark Butterfield has to be leery of this trap. He may believe that Mike O'Malley is politically powerful in the community. When Mark is faced with the decision regarding the inference by O'Malley, Mark has to be sure that he does not let his self-interests cloud his judgment. It is the self-interest criterion that frequently comes back to haunt the supervisor and often is responsible for termination.

Stress is another cognitive takeoff that is related to the idealized image. Stress is a part of the life of the supervisor. Researchers tell us that too much stress is related to poor decisions. There is an optimum level of stress related to decision making. Once that level is passed, the quality of decision making decreases. Mark cannot control stress or stressful situations.

TIP

Asking questions is a critical step to improving decision making.

Stressful situations can be created by the lack of time to adequately resolve a situation. There may be intense pressure brought to bear on an issue by a political group, a conflict between groups within the organization, or unpredicted situations. Even if the situation were predictable, reactions to the situation are unpredictable. When Mark finds himself in stressful situations he will be acting prudently if he can "stall" for time while he collects data, seeks the opinion of others, and generates a wide array of alternative solutions. There are some situations where a decision has to be made. Mark needs to recognize when a decision has to be made and when a decision can be safely postponed.

Mark needs to develop an internal locus of control. It is the locus of control that enables Mark to differentiate between a problem demanding an immediate response and an ego-driven demand to make a decision immediately. In the latter case, the decision is made to satisfy emotional needs. On the other hand, some situations demand a response. A teacher observes black-and-blue marks on a child's arm. The teacher has no choice but to report a suspected case of abuse. Here, the *heuristic* is clear. *Always follow the legal course of action.* A *heuristic* is a rule of thumb to use in stressful situations. It needs to be *value* driven. The heuristics Mark employs should be understandable to others, communicate a sense of values, and fit the community's moral and normative structure. Mark Butterfield can use a heuristic when he is pressured to make a decision regarding the status of the four players from Justin High School.

Some cognitive takeoffs are *affiliative* in nature. That is, they deal with relationships. These takeoffs are exemplified by the desire for *consensus, social approval,* and *acceptance. Consensus* affects decision-making when the object of discussion becomes consensus and not the quality of the decision.

Consensus groups are deeply involved in process. However, the need for consensus can limit vision and lead to poor decisions. President John Kennedy lamented, "How could I be so stupid!" when referring to his decision to support the invasion of Cuba. President Kennedy's advisors were in consensus that it was the right decision. Some advisors later describe their own feelings as knowing that the decision was wrong but being caught up in the group's desire to support the president.

When Mark places the need for social approval above the quality of the decision, he will make a decision for all the wrong reasons. Mark may be driven by a strong desire to have a superordinate bless his decision. He may expect similar approval from subordinates. In either case, Mark may *frame* his decision in the context of approval from his referencing group. These are politically correct decisions. Mark Butterfield could make such a decision by capitulating to the demands of Mike O'Malley. O'Malley would see his decision as good, yet it would be a poor decision. The role of the effective supervisor is fraught with isolation. It is isolating when the supervisor has to walk away from the social approval that is always waiting when decisions are made in the selfish interests of the crowd or powerful people. Making the right decision limits Mark's social approval.

Social acceptance is different from social approval in that social acceptance looks to the group for inclusion. It is a relationship that Mark may desire to make with the group. The decision affirms the group's normative structure. If Mark chooses not accept the group's normative structure, he should realize that the group will oppose his decision. Social approval is individual. Here Mark may look to those who are close in relationship. It may be his wife, parent, friend, or a significant other who approves or disapproves of him. There can be immense pressure placed on Mark from these people, since they provide strong emotional support. In Mark's mind, even if the organization turned against him, he would still have this close group of intimate relationships who would be supportive. For example, Mark Butterfield's wife may be best friends with Mike O'Malley's wife. During conversations, the two may talk at length about the coming playoffs. Mark's wife may see nothing wrong with following the normal grade-reporting procedure. This will place pressure on Mark from an unexpected source.

REFLECTION

How can you limit the influence of those whose social acceptance you need from interfering with your responsibility?

THE DECISION-MAKING PROCESS

The decision-making process has three distinct categories: problem identification, decision processing, and decision selection and implementation. Mark's understanding of this process will enable him to increase the likelihood of making good decisions.

PROBLEM IDENTIFICATION

Problem identification is crucial to the decision-making process. If the problem is not properly identified, then a correct decision cannot be made. Most difficulties related to decision making are made during this phase. Many supervisors are unaware of the problem that they are trying to solve. They have the good intent of making a decision that resolves the issue, but become frustrated because their best efforts do not resolve the problem. Unaware of the decision-making process, they address the problem's symptoms. It is small wonder that they repeatedly need to resolve the same problem. To solve the correct problem, Mark has to be aware of the problem's *symptoms, causes,* and *sources.* Mark can think of this situation in medical terms. A patient goes to a doctor with a complaint that he or she is experiencing fatigue. The doctor, only thinking of the symptoms, prescribes rest. The patient returns home and follows the doctor's advice. Two months later the patient is dead, the result of a disease the doctor did not identify because the doctor only recognized the symptoms. Symptoms are important. However, Mark needs to look beyond the symptoms and determine the causes and source. When Mark addresses the source, he is able to eliminate the symptoms.

The *causes* are easily identified. Consider the teacher who refers too many students to the office for discipline. This teacher may not have adequate classroom management skills. The symptom is the high number of student referrals to the office. However, the cause is the teacher's lack of classroom management skills. The supervisor, recognizing the symptom, begins to work with the teacher on the improvement of classroom management skills. The teacher cooperates but does not internalize the supervisor's guidance, since the teacher believes that the problem is in the children and the community. In 3 weeks, the number of referrals from the teacher begins to climb. The supervisor becomes frustrated and begins a case of documentation to eliminate the teacher from the district's workforce. The supervisor did not consider the *source* of the problem.

The *source* of the problem is the underlying substructure of the cause and symptoms. If the sources to this underlying substructure are effectively addressed, then the symptoms will be eradicated on a permanent basis. In this case, the supervisor may identify three possible sources for the large number of discipline referrals by the teacher. The first possible source is the teacher's attitude toward discipline. Is the teacher's attitude a personality characteristic or is it generated by the teacher's preparation program? Second, the supervisor needs to consider the district's teacher selection process. Is the selection process so weak that the district is unable to keep poor teachers from being hired? And third, is the university that prepared this teacher at fault? Perhaps all the teachers from this university have similar problems. The source may be one of the above, or it may be a combination of all three. The source of the problem is best found by asking the right questions.

REFLECTION

What major problem exists in your work unit? What are its symptoms? Can you identify the cause? What is the source of the cause(s) and symptoms?

DECISION PROCESSING

The *decision processing* stage has several phases that Mark must follow if he desires to increase his probability of making a good decision. There are many good decision-process models. Each of the models can enable Mark to make a better decision. However, nearly every model has the same components (Fig. 3.2).

FIGURE 3.2. DECISION-MAKING MODEL

Step 1: Identification of the problem.

Step 2: Collection of information that is directly relevant to the problem.

Step 3: Establishment of solution criteria.

Step 4: Generation of alternatives.

Step 5: Weighing of alternatives against the criteria.

Step 6: Selection of the best alternative.

Step 7: Consideration of the consequences of the chosen course.

Step 8: Implementation of the chosen solution.

Step 9: Evaluation of the solution.

Step 10: Modification of the implemented solution.

The first step is the *identification of the problem*. This step was covered in the identification of the symptoms, causes, and sources of the problem. The second part of making a decision, *decision processing,* includes collection of information relevant to the problem, establishment of solution criteria, generation of alternatives, and weighing of alternatives against the criteria.

The second step is the collection of information relevant to the problem. Mark needs to collect information to help him confirm the causes and sources of the problem. Mark must discipline himself to reject extraneous information. The amount of relative information that Mark collects is directly proportional to the amount of time that he has to make the decision. There comes a point, in each decision-making process, where Mark has to conclude that he has collected sufficient data to make a decision. Before this point is reached, Mark has to make sure that the search is substantive and not superficial.

For example, Mark Butterfield, prior to making the decision regarding the eligibility of the four players, needs to collect information. He needs to check with the school board regarding policy, check with the state athletic association that governs interscholastic play, and check past practice in the district regarding this issue. Notice, Mark is not checking on political solutions. He is not asking for opinions. He is **collecting data**. Too often, supervisors fall into the trap of collecting opinions rather than data at this preliminary stage. As a result, they make political decisions rather than correct decisions. Once Mark is armed with the data, he can present them to the principal and the booster club president. Frequently, the data will make the decision.

The third step is in the establishment of solution criteria. Mark needs to determine the criteria for an effective solution to each of his problems. He should ask, "What would this situation look like if it were resolved?" "What are the characteristics that I want to see in an implemented solution?" This type of thinking will help him to be more focused when he generates alternatives.

Mark may find a solution to the Justin High School issue with a specific policy approved by the school board which addresses this issue. Mark then refers to this policy each time someone asks him an eligibility question. The establishment of criteria is not the solution. It is the standard for the solution.

The fourth step is the generation of alternatives. Decision-making quality is enhanced when Mark is willing to generate, through discussion with others, a wide range of alternative solutions. The greater the number of solutions generated, the higher the probability that Mark will make the correct decision. This is an *optimizing* strategy as opposed to a *satisficing* strategy. In the latter case, the first viable alternative is chosen and the search for a solution ceases. In the former case, the search is exhaustive for alternatives. In this search, no alternative is considered useless. They are all considered valid. The only criterion used is that the alternatives are technologically feasible and that, if selected, are implementable in a timely fashion. Russell Ackoff has called this "idealized design" and has written extensively on this topic.[3]

The fifth step is the weighing of alternatives against the criteria. In this stage, each alternative is listed and assessed as to how well it meets the criteria. For example, Mark Butterfield has criteria for a good solution that includes meeting (1) legal requirements, (2) state athletic association requirements, (3) school board policy, (4) high ethical standards, and (5) giving academic standards priority over athletic success. These standards eliminate the solutions offered by the principal and Mike O'Malley. The use of standards gives Mark added strength when explaining a decision. The standards are rational, detached, and fair.

The sixth step is the selection of the best alternative. Mark must consider any new information. Once Mark is assured that he has all available information, he can begin the selection process. Mark has a number of competing alternatives. One way he can successfully choose the best alternative is to use the decision-making process termed *elimination by objectives*. In

[3] Russell Ackhoff, *Creating the Corporate Future: Planned or Be Planned For*. New York: John Wiley & Sons (1981).

elimination by objectives, an alternative is eliminated if it does not meet previously established criteria. Mark may set a standard that his decisions must comply with state regulations governing athletics. This standard automatically eliminates alternatives that violate state guidelines.

The seventh step is the consideration of the consequences of the alternatives. It is here that Mark tries to understand the risks and benefits involved in each. Mark has to assess the cost of the solution. If Mark Butterfield chooses to follow the principal's advice, the risk factor may include forfeiture of the game at a later date, his termination, and/or a public relations black eye for the school district. On the other hand, if he chooses to go with an alternative that does not allow the students to play, he risks the loss of the Boosters' Club's support. Decisions are not easy. However, once Mark understands the risks of each alternative he becomes more aware of what he is doing. Being aware of his decisions and their consequences enables Mark to choose the best course of action.

Once the alternatives and their risks have been assessed, Mark should use his intuition. Mark needs to consider the two highest rated alternatives, pause for reflection, and then choose a single solution by allowing the intuiting process to search the right hemisphere of his brain for insight. Mark's subconscious is continually active. He needs to comprehend what his subconscious mind has discovered. Mark's insight may appear as a *hunch* or *gut*. If Mark couples his insight with a solid decision-making process, he will make a good decision.

REFLECTION

Do you rely on intuition that is formed by data? Do you trust your instinctual judgments?

Implementation is the eighth step. Implementation takes planning, involvement, and coordination. Part of the implementation process is informing people of the decision and its impact on their lives. In medical terminology, this process is called *stress inoculation*. *Stress inoculation* is the preparation of people for the potential consequences of a decision. Researchers have discovered that patients who are accurately forewarned of how they will respond to surgery have a significantly higher healing rate than those who are not forewarned. In each decision that Mark makes, his chances for success are increased if he communicates the reasons for his decision and the risk factors associated with the decision. In this way, he prepares those whom his decision affects to adapt to a changing scene.

The ninth step is decision evaluation. Mark needs to evaluate his decisions. He evaluates his decisions on the basis of their outcomes. Some decisions turn out poorly. These consequences need to be recognized early in the implementation process. This is done through continued monitoring and assessment of the implemented solution. *Benchmarks* are set to measure intermittent progress or gauge a negative direction. A standard should clearly sound an alarm to halt the decision implementation. These are prudent and effective safeguards. If the results of the decision are positive, Mark can consider his decision as successful and continue its implementation. The decision-making process is fraught with traps. The most serious of traps are the ones that we set for ourselves. These are the traps that are formed because of biases, hidden decision-making styles, and information filters. If it were not for these traps, there would be no poor decisions. Supervisors have a responsibility to make good decisions. They have a responsibility to each member of their unit and to all who are connected with their unit. The supervisor's decision-making ability impacts the success or lack of success of their unit.

REFLECTION

Have any of your supervisors failed to evaluate a decision? What happened when the decision turned out poorly?

PULLING IT TOGETHER

FIELD BASED PROJECTS

1. Conduct a focus group composed of teachers in your school related to the decision-making process. Ask the teachers how involved they are in the decision-making process. Ask them to reflect on the decision-making processes of their immediate supervisors. Ask them for recommendations that would improve the quality of decision making at their work site.

2. Identify the five most important decisions that were made in your organization in the past year. Chart the process that was used to make these decisions. Determine who was involved in the implementation process, and gather as much information as possible related to the evaluation of these decisions. If no evaluation has been formerly conducted ask those associated with the decision the reasons for not evaluating the decision.

3. Shadow a supervisor in your organization for a day. Record each decision that the supervisor makes. Most supervisors will make hundreds of decisions each day. Determine if you can identify the heuristics that the supervisor is using to guide his or her decision-making process. Each time the supervisor makes a decision, record the decision that you would have made. How do your decisions compare with those of the supervisor? At the end of the day reflect on the decisions that the supervisor made, note questions that you have, and share these thoughts with the supervisor. Determine if the supervisor had available

information to make a decision of which you were not aware.

FIELD BASED ANALYSIS

1. Conduct a needs assessment that involves parents, students, and teachers regarding the quality of decisions that are made by administrators in your school district. Analyze the results for trends. Determine from your data whether the assessment of those taking the needs assessment is based on the quality of the decision or their personal philosophy regarding decisions.

2. Interview five supervisors in your work organization. Ask each supervisor to explain how decisions are made in his or her unit. Once you have completed these interviews, interview members of these units and ask them to explain how decisions are made in their unit. Compare the members' perception with the perception of the supervisor. How do you account for differences?

3. Gain permission to sit in on meetings of your organization's decision-making council. This may be a site-based decision-making team or an administrative council. Observe the decision-making process. Determine if the decision-making process uses an optimizing or satisficing strategy. Is the group open to new ideas or does group think prevail? Once a decision is made, how is it implemented? Is responsibility for implementation assigned?

IF YOU WERE MARK BUTTERFIELD...

How would you respond to Mike O'Malley?

How would you respond to the principal at Justin High School?

How would you determine if games were to be played?

How would you respond to criticism for canceling the games when the storm never materialized?

How would you prioritize the problems that you face?

How would you relate to those who demand instant decisions (reactors)?

How would you prevent "group think" from driving your decisions?

What data would you consider essential to make effective decisions?

What are the decisions that are required of you?

What are the alternatives that you can generate for each decision that you have to make?

What would be your decision in each of the circumstances that requires a decision from you?

How would you *stress inoculate* your constituencies regarding your decisions?

How would you communicate your decisions?

How would you respond to the parents of the student athletes if you did not allow them to play?

RESOURCES FOR SUPERVISORS
BOOKS

Bell, D., Raiffa, H., Tversky, A. (eds.). *Descriptive, Normative and Prescriptive Infections.* New York: Cambridge (1988).

Heller, F. (ed.). *Decision Making and Leadership.* New York: Cambridge (1992).

WEB SITE

http://edweb.cnidr.org.90/ (This web site explores the worlds of educational reform and information technology.)

4

SUCCEEDING AT CHANGE
FOR SUPERVISORS

BUILDING BLOCKS

Promotion
Encouragement
Risk-Taking
Assessment

INTRODUCTION

Earlier we developed the metaphor of the supervisor as scout. A scout is a person who goes ahead of the group carefully exploring the trail, looking for signs of danger and places of shelter. While scouting, supervisors discover aspects of a unit that need to be modified, bolstered, or aligned. When these aspects are altered, change occurs. In this chapter, you learn how to be a change agent.

Change represents going from the safety of the known to the insecurity of the unknown. Change is a source of stress as organizational members struggle to control the direction of the change. That direction can be new or it can be a return to practices of years past. In any event, change is a source of turmoil that needs to be managed by the supervisor. Supervisors who initiate change are referred to as change agents. Frequently, the supervisor, as change agent, is driven by a transforming vision that cannot be seen or understood in its present form by the members of the organization. Yet, the supervisor's will to pursue this course will alter the members' work and the organization's environment.

Supervisors face challenges as they attempt to create an environment wherein constructive change thrives. Through the scouting skills learned previously, the supervisor recognizes the new programs or policies that need to be developed to focus the activities and efforts of the unit's people to move the organization in a new direction. Once areas of change are recognized, the supervisor needs to carefully construct a strategic change plan. The development of this plan takes time, energy, patience, and specialized skills. As you read this chapter, examine the various concepts presented. Reflect on the actions of the person in the supervision situation. Ask yourself, "What should the supervisor do?" and, "How should the supervisor do it?"

SUPERVISION SITUATION

Anne Lester completed her first year as principal of Latrobe High School. She was satisfied with the progress the faculty and students had made. However, she was deeply concerned over the high number of students who did not
complete their high school education. Her school's dropout
rate was the highest in the city. This was unacceptable to the
community and to Anne.

During the latter part of the school year, Anne worked
with the counseling staff to review data that related to the at-
risk population. They discovered that the dropout rates had
significantly increased. They were able to pinpoint some common characteristics among the at-risk population. Typically,
the students who were at-risk were not involved in extracurricular programs and activities. They scored below average on
state-mandated tests. The majority of the students who
dropped out had not been assigned to a first-period class or
homeroom period when they dropped out of school. These
students started their day during the second period. Anne's
predecessor implemented a staggered schedule to cope with
overcrowding conditions. Anne discovered that the school
coped with the overcrowding by staggering the time school
started, eliminating study halls for juniors and seniors, eliminating homeroom periods for juniors and seniors, and reduc-
ing the number of minutes in the last period. Ironically, the
district's enrollment reversed and her school saw a drop in enrollment. Even though the conditions changed, the plan to
cope with overenrollment continued to drive the school schedule. Teachers and counselors used this "window of time" to
develop enrichment tutorials for gifted and talented students.

Anne checked with the superintendent to see if the school
was obligated to keep the staggered schedule since it was no
longer needed. The superintendent agreed to support Anne's
efforts to use the school schedule to address the dropout
problem. Anne proceeded with her plans to change the current
school schedule to the traditional 8:15 AM to 3:30 PM schedule

and to require both a first period class and a homeroom period for all students. Anne shared this information with her team. The team advised Anne to inform the faculty so that the faculty could be allowed to participate in the change. Anne was wary of a potential political struggle. She decided to wait until meeting with the faculty for the final time before the summer recess. In the meantime, word leaked out to the faculty that Anne was going to "unilaterally" alter the school schedule. When Anne announced her changes at the faculty meeting she was met with silence and then unified faculty opposition to her plans.

REFLECTION

How would you have the addressed the issue of the student dropout rate differently than Anne?

RESISTANCE TO CHANGE

There are members in every organization who resist change. Frequently, those who resist change are the people who conform to established ways of thinking, existing practices, procedures, and policies. These people are satisfied with the status quo. It provides a sense of emotional security to them. In one sense, there is a constant struggle between the "pioneer" (change agent) and the "settler" (the person desiring the status quo). Both types of people are needed in an organization. If an organization were constantly in the pioneer state, there would be nothing that members could use as a foundation. On the other hand, if the organization were constantly in the settler state, members would not adapt to changing environmental demands. Anne's faculty are settlers. They found security with the existing schedule, established programs, and carved-out activities. These settlers pose the most difficult challenge for Anne as she initiates movement toward pioneer status. Before Anne brings these settlers to the desire to move, she has to recognize and understand why they fear change.

Merrill and Donna Douglas[1] cite several reasons why people fear and resist change:

LACK OF INPUT INTO CHANGE

Effective supervisors know that subordinates will not embrace and support change if they are not part of the process. Involvement needs to start with identification of issues, brainstorming solutions, and narrowing alternatives.

NEGATIVE EXPERIENCES ASSOCIATED WITH CHANGE

Comfort can be found with the known and discomfort with the unknown. Humans tend to be "creatures of habit" and find change in routines unsettling. Because of the unsettling nature of change and the pain that is associated with the processes of change, people resist efforts to move from the settler role to the pioneer role. Anne's efforts to prepare the staff for the pioneer role must include education, support, and encouragement of the faculty. Her commitment to this process will reduce the stress associated with change and gain widespread support for her efforts. If Anne lacks this commitment, she reinforces the negative memories that many of the staff have that are associated with schedule changes.

CHANGE IS A THREAT TO SECURITY

Change produces fears associated with job security. Often change is associated with demands to learn new skills or processes of accomplishing unit objectives. If a subordinate associates evaluation with change, the anxiety level increases and the change is a threat to future employment. Effective supervisors nurture people to eliminate their fears about change. For example, the faculty in Anne's school may see the new schedule as a means to eliminate staff. Then they will frame the su-

---

[1] Merril E. Douglas and Donna N. Douglas, *Time Management for Teams.* New York: American Management Association (1992), p. 10.

perintendent's support for the change as a way to reduce the instructional salaries budget rather than as a way to reduce the dropout rate.

JOB SATISFACTION IS REDUCED BY CHANGE

Herzberg's job satisfaction research shows that the work environment itself is a strong motivator for increased satisfaction. Once the work environment begins to change, subordinates feel unsure of their place. Anne can reduce this anxiety by communicating the reasons for the potential changes and the possible outcomes, both good and bad. Anne, by communicating frequently and in clearly understood terms regarding her proposed changes before, during, and after a change has occurred, will reduce her staff's level of anxiety.

TIMING AND ASSOCIATED WORK

Anne needs to consider the timing of her change strategies. There are times when change is inappropriate because of the high level of stress that is seasonally associated with her faculty. For example, a retailer would not want to introduce major changes to floor clerks during the holiday shopping season. Similarly, Anne would not want to introduce major changes during peak demand times on her staff. Effective supervisors understand the peak-times concept and give it strong consideration when considering change initiatives.

THE NEED FOR CHANGE

Change is a part of the teaching experience. Anne has to develop a case to present to her faculty that change is necessary. One error Anne made was her assumption that she had ownership of the sole correct direction. Decision-making literature tells us that there may be many equally effective alternatives. If Anne were willing to enter into a shared problem-solving and diagnosis process with her staff, the faculty would develop a better understanding of the need for the change and potentially develop a series of options different from Anne's original concept. Collectively, Anne and her faculty see the need and benefit of change.

THE PROACTIVE NATURE OF CHANGE

Effective supervisors proactively approach change. Effective supervisors are able to communicate personal and organizational benefits as the underlying reason for initiating change. Self-interest is a primary motivating factor for most people. When the supervisor links the organization's self-interests to that of the unit member, then the unit member is likely to see the need for change. Anne's willingness to embrace the call of the superintendent and school board member for stronger evaluation policies can only be viewed by the faculty as Anne working in her own best interests. Anne can counteract this negative faculty perception by demonstrating to the faculty that improved evaluation procedures are in the faculty's best interests.

TRUST IS AN ESSENTIAL ELEMENT OF CHANGE

Trust is an essential component of effective change. Subordinates need to trust their supervisors. We suggest you return to Chapter 1 to review effective supervisory traits and behaviors. Presence of these traits yields higher levels of trust for supervisors. Trust is an earned characteristic. It is not one that Anne has as a result of being named principal. Anne earns the trust of her faculty by each of her actions. The faculty will ask themselves, either consciously or subconsciously, Is Anne doing this for me? Or, Is Anne doing this to promote her own self-interests?

REFLECTION

Have you had to undergo change at your workplace where there was little trust in the supervisor?
How successful was the change? How did you respond to the supervisor?

INCREASE THE LEVEL OF PARTICIPATION IN CHANGE DISCUSSIONS

Anne's scouting skills led her to data that gave possible
reasons for the increased dropout rate. She allowed limited
participation in the process by only involving the members of
her administrative team. When Anne includes members of the
faculty in the planning process, she moves in the right direction. However, Anne made a tactical error. She involved a
limited number of people in the data collection and analysis
process. The changes she was considering had a potential impact well beyond this limited team. A change in the schedule
will change the way teachers and students interact with one
another; the way the work day is configured; the lives of students; the fast-food restaurants which depend on the juniors
and seniors as consumers and workers; and the ways in which
teachers have their workday scheduled. Those who are not
involved in the decision-making process have a need to be involved and hear Anne's explanation before she changes the
schedule. She didn't involve them directly in the decision-
making process, consult with them to discover their feelings
regarding the proposed changes, or consider a wide array of
other suitable alternatives to the one solution chosen.

Initiating change is difficult when people do not understand the need for change. Many attempts at change fail because the supervisor fails to consider the educational component inherent in successful change efforts. Anne needs to educate the Latrobe High School educational community. Shirley
Hord suggests that change is a process, not an event. Since

change is a process, Anne needs to exhibit leadership in managing this change. As a process, time is needed for teachers, students, and parents to assimilate the need for the proposed change. This process has to be planned in a logical, left-brained, linear fashion.

CHANGE IS A COMPLEX PHENOMENON

Change is a complex process which takes place over a period of time. Anne's efforts to change the school schedule to affect the dropout rate have immediate and long-term implications. Depending on the consequences of the change, the long-term implications will negatively or positively affect the school. Anne needs to be aware of each of these consequences. Her proposed change may have a positive impact on the dropout rate. That is good. However, it may have a negative impact on the gifted and talented students. If Anne does not process the consequences of the change, she may create problems that had not previously existed.

CHANGE IS ACCOMPLISHED BY PEOPLE

Anne can accomplish long-lasting and systemic change with the support of her faculty. Because change is a highly personal experience, the teachers at Latrobe need to be able to internalize the change and reconcile what this change means. Anne needs to remain objective and calm as people express concerns and objections to the proposed change. Anne can foster open communication and ongoing dialogue by not being offended by criticism. Anne can find herself defending her position and losing objectivity. Once Anne loses her objectivity, she loses credibility with the faculty. This leads to change becoming a political issue rather than an educational issue. When change becomes a political issue, winners and losers are born. The end result is never positive. Celebrations in these circumstances always leave the losers on the sidelines waiting their turn at revenge.

CHANGE CAUSES ANXIETY

Change can cause anxiety. When change is about to occur, people face the unknown. The known is more comforting. Anne needs to determine if she understands the psychological impact the proposed change has on the affected groups. The psychological impact can be determined, in part, by understanding the organization's history. From such an understanding comes common ground from where Anne and her faculty can begin. Anne also needs to examine her motivations. Is Anne motivated by the high number of students dropping out of school, or is she equally motivated by the superintendent and board of education's wish to cut costs by altering the master schedule? If Annie's motivation is personal, she will have problems with her teachers. They will see her selfish interests.

REFLECTION

Describe a recent change at your workplace and the anxiety that accompanied this change. What would you have done to reduce the level of anxiety?

PREPARING FOR CHANGE

Anne needs to develop a plan to initiate the change process. Anne knows she needs to take the lead in initiating this change. Before developing a plan, however, Anne should consider the type of change that is needed by her school.

TYPES OF CHANGE

Friedman and Yarbrough believe there are two primary types of change that occur within organizations: *first order change* and *second order change*.

First order change occurs within a system which itself remains unchanged. Because first order change can be likened to window dressing or change for change's sake, it is the least effective type of change. On the other hand, *second order change* deals with changing the aspects of the system which are weak. This type of change is more effective because it is systemic.

If Anne and her teachers change the master schedule, they will be engaging in *first order change* because they are not considering the conditions that cause students to dropout. Changing the master schedule will not encourage or motivate teachers to focus on student retention. On the other hand, if Anne and her teachers view the schedule as part of the interrelated systemic components, then they will see the schedule changes as a part of the change process and not the process itself.

It takes time to prepare an organization for change. Kurt Lewin called the process of readying an organization for change *unfreezing*. During unfreezing, the supervisor and the community develop a readiness for change. It is during this period that the organization experiencing change begins to acquire the skills necessary for change to occur. During this *unfreezing* period, much of Anne's time and energy needs to focus on building trust, showing the concrete results to be achieved, anticipating obstacles to be faced, and readying the people and organization for them. After considering these aspects, Anne needs to guide her organization through the change. The following steps are a guide to this process.

STEP 1: FACE CHANGE OPENLY AND PUBLICLY

Anne can meet with groups of teachers, students, and parents to determine their underlying fears and concerns. The information gained through these meetings will assist Anne in developing a strategy to address change.

STEP 2: PROVIDE DATA

Anne educates her community most effectively by the objective dissemination of pertinent data, not through emotional rhetoric. The data, both pro and con, should substantiate

Anne's case. If Anne does not present all of the data, but uses only that part that supports her rationale, she demonstrates a lack of integrity. However, the data should be informative to Anne as well as to her constituents. Perhaps Anne will be open-minded and reconsider her change mission if the data suggest that there are other more demanding reasons for the increase in the dropout rate.

STEP 3: USE THE PARETO PRINCIPLE

The Pareto principle suggests that Anne should expend 80% of her energy on the 20% of the faculty who make the difference. It also suggests that 20% of her faculty will not support her initiative—even if it is beneficial to them. Anne's focus of energy on the 20% who make the difference will eventually gain the support of the remaining 60% of the faculty who choose to sit on the sidelines and withhold support or objections until they see the consequences of the change. Anne needs to make sure she accurately targets the correct group.

TIP

Take the time to use the Pareto principle. It will save time in the long run.

USE OF AUTHORITY AND CHANGE

By virtue of her position, Anne has legitimate authority. She has the right and duty to challenge her faculty to meet high standards of performance. However, the use of authority is a two-sided coin. Anne can use her authority to promote her cause. Or she can use her authority in the best interests of her constituents. While planning for and implementing change, it is critical for Anne to garner goodwill and momentum for change, which cannot be achieved through coercive means. How Anne challenges the faculty reflects her values about the role of faculty in the decision-making and change processes.

LEADERSHIP THEORIES

Douglas McGregor describes two distinctly different leadership theories, *Theory X* and *Theory Y*. *Theory Y* leaders display democratic leadership behaviors because they believe subordinates are capable of directing their own work. These leaders have self-control, are creative, and strive for excellence and high quality work. *Theory Y* leaders inspire people to do their best. Motivation is provided through empowerment and opportunities for participation in such areas as decision-making and change. *Theory Y* leaders respect and value their subordinates, and the ideas that they bring to the context.

Conversely, *Theory X* leaders lead by control, excessive rules and regulations, and minimization of the contributions of subordinates. The contributions of subordinates are seldom valued, and subordinates are not empowered to set organizational direction. Participation in decision-making and change is nonexistent. *Theory X* leaders take care of details because they lack faith in their subordinates' ability to perform.

Effective supervisors are *Theory Y* driven. They believe in the innate capacity of the members of their organization to succeed. They believe that people want to be successful and productive. To the extent that Anne is *Theory Y* driven, she will provide guidance, leadership, and motivation to challenge and inspire her faculty. In this sense, she will use her authority legitimately in the best interests of her constituents. As a result, her faculty will support her initiatives. This will cause a buildup in momentum that provides continuous energy for the change action.

REFLECTION

Describe your current supervisor. Is this person a *Theory X* or *Theory Y* supervisor? Which type do you prefer to work with; explain.

Robert Rosen has suggested that leaders need to navigate the change process by "continually challenging the organization to keep the momentum going."[2] To challenge her faculty, Anne needs to create a culture and climate in her building that strengthens the organization's structure. To do this, Anne needs to support creative activities by promoting participation in making critical decisions about the organization. Increased participation enhances the development of working relationships between and among subordinates and administrators. However, increased participation requires Anne to validate her faculty's work and champion the efforts of faculty members who have taken risks and failed. To ease the work and increase involvement in change, Anne needs to meet regularly with her faculty to facilitate their work and to help them set and keep reasonable goals.

ADVOCATING CHANGE

Anne needs to become the advocate for the proposed change. As the primary advocate for her proposed change, Anne must commit to significant planning time. Anne needs to use her influence as a leader to show how the change benefits the community. An important aspect in advocating for change is *establishing a need*. In his book, *Teaching the Elephant to Dance*, James Belasco underscores the power of recognizing and acting upon the needs of an organization when attempting to enact change. Belasco believes that organizations—people and structures—change slowly unless there is an understood and identified need. These needs, however elusive, must be discovered. Anne needs to help her teachers recognize their school's needs and through collective action commit to change. Anne's plan should include these steps:

---

[2] Robert H. Rosen with Paul B. Brown, *Transforming Business From the Inside Out: Leading People*. New York: Penguin Group (1996), p. 56.

STEP 1: KEEP THE CHANGE PROCESS OPEN

Anne needs to share her information with her faculty. Information helps allay fears, squelch rumors, and put people on the same footing. Information is power; when people are receiving information, they are sharing in power. Anne shares power when she shares essential information.

STEP 2: ASK FOR HELP

Change does not take place in a vacuum. Anne needs to ask for advice. In seeking advice, Anne needs to be an active listener. When she actively listens, Anne becomes a primary learner. Her sources of learning should be expansive and move beyond the boundaries of her school to the community and to experts in the area of scheduling and at-risk students.

STEP 3: FORM FOCUS GROUPS

Focus groups assist Anne in identifying the emotions associated with the proposed change. Anne needs to listen to the emotions as well as the words of those participating in the focus groups. Calabrese, Short, and Zepeda describe the mechanisms needed to run a successful focus group in *Hands-On Leadership Tools for Principals* (Larchmont, NY: Eye On Education (1996)).

STEP 4: LINK EFFORTS AND RESOURCES TO THE CHANGE

As Anne develops her strategic plan to implement change, she considers how each school-related activity (e.g., staff development, in-service, school improvement plan development) supports the change process. Successful change links these activities to create a central focus. It is this central focus which captures the attention of the school community. Failure to focus creates the dispersal of energy and attention. When attention is dispersed, various foci compete for primacy, with no central issue gaining primacy.

STEP 5: ASSESSMENT

Anne needs to assess the change process by establishing a series of benchmarks. Each benchmark corresponds to a critical phase of the change process. Some benchmarks are faculty involvement, dissemination of information, education of the community, feedback, and target focusing. Each time Anne assesses a benchmark, she is able to course-correct her change process. At each benchmark, Anne sets the criteria for the assessment of that benchmark for future reference. For example, Anne sets faculty involvement in the change process at 40%. She has specific criteria as to what "involvement" means. She has a sub-benchmark for direct and indirect involvement. If she has not met these goals, Anne needs to stop and develop new strategies to increase involvement and set a new date to reassess the *involvement* benchmark.

MINIMIZING ANXIETY

Earlier in this chapter, we urged you to examine the *history of change* to determine levels of anxiety. The examination of past practice helps Anne to understand the sources of her faculty's anxiety. Anxiety is caused by not understanding the potential outcome of the proposed change. Once Anne is aware of the sources of the faculty's anxiety, she addresses that problem. The source of her faculty's anxiety may be their lack of involvement in the change process by previous administrations. Once she understands the source, Anne can develop strategies to counteract the anxiety.

There are a series of strategies that Anne can implement to reduce the level of her faculty's anxiety. Anne's faculty members need reassurance that their status will not be dramatically altered as a result of her proposed change. If it is significantly altered, they need to be reassured that Anne will assist them in the transitional period as they adjust to their new role. Anne can reduce anxiety by actively involving the individuals in charting shifts in roles, status, and responsibilities once the change has been initiated.

Anne can work with her faculty to plan training, skill development, and ongoing support. Through monitoring activities, effective supervisors provide the resources for training and ongoing support once a change is in process. Training and ongoing support throughout change cannot be underscored enough. Throughout this process, her faculty needs to have their work history endorsed and to focus on future contributions to future personal and organizational growth. Anne can help her faculty resist the temptation to attach the need for change to condemnation of present efforts. She will need strong communication and political skills (see Chapter 8).

There are many reasons why anxiety exists. (For further information, refer to Leonard Laskow's *Healing Love* (San Francisco: Harper Collins, 1992).) Anne needs to discover these reasons and move to address them before she continues. These reasons can be considered barriers. The following are six powerful barriers.

BARRIER 1: UNWILLINGNESS TO MAKE A COMMITMENT

Commitment is a personal issue, yet it has tremendous organizational consequences. Commitment is a public response to a private demand. The public response requires action on the part of the person making the commitment. A person or group that gives its public response is more likely to work for an issue to which it is committed. Anne needs to solicit public commitment. In soliciting public commitment, she cannot shy away from publicly asking, "Are you willing to commit yourself to this process?" The question is asked individually, in the presence of other people. Anne now knows how willing her faculty is to move in the direction of the desired change. A public commitment provides the fortitude that a group or person needs when faced with difficulties.

BARRIER 2: CONCERN OVER LOSS OF CONTROL

Human beings enjoy predictability. Change is unpredictability. Unpredictable means, for many, the loss of control over their present circumstances. Generally, when people feel that they do not have control over their environment, they resist change. This means that Anne has to guide the faculty in the process, pointing out benchmarks that they can grab hold of for security. Each benchmark gives them a sense of control, something that they use as an anchor. Some faculty have little need for control, while others need an inordinate sense of control over their destiny. Anne must recognize individual differences so that she can encourage and support those who have difficulty with little control and stay out of the way of those who do not need control.

BARRIER 3: REMEMBERING

Remembering becomes a barrier when the faculty recalls failed changes under different administrators. They may make erroneous assumptions that all change is bad or that all supervisors make changes poorly. Anne can overcome this process through small chunks of success. This is accomplished one step at a time where the faculty sees the success. These small chunks of success serve as a source of reconstructing the remembering process and replacing negative memories associated with change with positive, constructive memories. This is a slow process. It is essential for future change to have a chance in Anne's school.

BARRIER 4: UNWILLINGNESS TO TRUST

Trust is a key component to organization or interpersonal success. If Anne cannot be trusted, she will not gain the support of her faculty. If she is trusted, she will have the commitment of her faculty. The failure to trust is personal. It is a sign that the person who does not trust has previously been betrayed or rejected. The depth of the betrayal and the pain associated with the betrayal are inversely proportional to the level of trust that the person can exhibit. It doesn't matter if Anne did not betray the faculty member. The betrayed person acts in a defense mode to protect himself or herself from future harm. Anne needs to gradually move toward those who find it difficult to trust. She cannot take their resistance personally. Her reaction, sense of integrity, and willingness to let them occasionally test her fidelity will gradually increase their levels of trust.

BARRIER 5: UNWILLINGNESS TO BECOME INVOLVED

Anne will have faculty who do not share her enthusiasm for work. These faculty may be good teachers, but have little desire to commit themselves to any activity beyond the classroom. There are several explanations for this lack of motivation. Some faculty may resist being connected with other faculty. Others may have a private sense of self and do not care to let people become too close. A fear of not being accepted, having ideas rejected, or a general sense of personal inadequacy may drive part of this motivation. Anne cannot force involvement. Anne can encourage involvement. Anne can gradually ease the process of involvement by creating safe havens for meetings. The more people involved, the deeper the commitment. However, the process of involvement cannot be rushed.

BARRIER 6: UNWILLINGNESS TO LET GO OF FRAMES

Each of Anne's faculty has a special window through which they see the world. This window presents a picture that makes emotional and psychological sense to them. It is a window that has been developed since birth. The views we see out of our windows are highly defended. When our windows are shattered, our perceptions of the world are shattered. It makes good sense to protect them from being shattered. Anne's strategy is not to point out the flaws in maladjusted views through each person's window. Her strategy is to widen the scope of their vision as they look out of their window. As the scope of their vision widens, faculty members broaden their perspective and become more inclusive. Anne broadens a faculty member's perspective by protecting the member's current perspective and gradually adding depth and breadth.

REFLECTION

What barriers currently exist in your workplace that interfere with the change process? Is it possible to eliminate these barriers?

Once Anne reduces the fear and apprehension associated with change, she moves at a more accelerated pace by developing a culture of risk-taking and adventure. Anne needs to adopt a "fault-free" environment to promotes taking risks. Some risks are calculated, and others are not. There is a thought that the higher the risk, the greater the results. Encouraging fault-free risk taking can reap benefits, increasing the willingness of subordinates to take risks. When Anne embraces the concept of risk taking, she empowers her faculty to risk. Risk taking becomes a cultural normative activity. Anne realizes that risk-taking can lead to failure. The faculty will carefully gauge her response to failure associated with risk. If she chooses to celebrate the failure, they will risk more readily. If she condemns the failure, they will be reluctant to risk in the future. Ineffective supervisors use scapegoats to project anger for risk-taking failures.

ENHANCING PERFORMANCE OF CHANGE PLAYERS

Anne can enhance the performance of those involved in the change process through understanding, patience, persistence, encouragement, and coaching. Anne practices understanding when she recognizes that resistance to change is not a personal issue. Only Anne can frame it in a win/lose context. Anne can resist the win/lose frame and move to the same side of the table to work with the resistant faculty members to understand the reasons for resistance. Once the "real" reasons are understood, the faculty member(s) and Anne can work cooperatively to address those issues.

Anne practices patience by allowing the faculty member latitude in his or her change options. Anne must recognize the difference between encouragement and pushing. There are times when Anne will have to push; however, the push can be done with assurances. Patience is a product which supervisors need. When they demonstrate patience toward the faculty, the faculty will often reciprocate and be patient with their supervisor.

REFLECTION

Describe a personal situation where you were impatient with the change process. Did change move too fast or too slowly?

Anne practices persistence by not allowing resistance to stifle her desire to move the organization forward. Anne needs to move in the direction of positive change one step at a time. She uses each step as a benchmark to recruit more allies, to demonstrate the efficacy of her actions, and to course correct. As the ancient Chinese proverb states, "A journey of a thousand miles begins with a single step." We ascribe to that philosophy and add that the journey is never really completed but progresses one step at a time.

Anne practices encouragement when she acts as a cheerleader to the members of her organization engaged in change. The most important act is focusing on a single positive act. If Anne can catch these single positive acts, she provides the faculty member with an anchor, a memory, or things that happen correctly. These anchors become the launching pads for future successes on the journey.

Anne coaches her faculty as they practice their new roles. She encouraged each member to step more deeply into the complexities of his or her new role and experiment with various unrehearsed strategies. Each step into a new and more demanding role, when accompanied by the steady hand of a coach, assures that positive actions are reinforced while inaccurate actions are "caught" and restructured to become positive actions. Change fails if the faculty member becomes frustrated with the new strategy and has no person to act as a coach in the process. It fails when the faculty member has no guide to show them "how to do it." A coach needs to be present during this process.

Galpin suggests nine guidelines for effective coaching during the change process: (1) Anne needs to inform her faculty that she will be coaching all members of the faculty. (2) Anne needs to make sure that her coaching is timely. The closer to the time of the activity she is able to coach behavior, the more effective the results of her instruction. (3) Anne has to realize that a good coach provides an environment wherein people want to be coached; it is a place where they are comfortable and are ready to receive feedback. (4) Anne must recognize the difference between coaching and criticism. Coaching focuses on improvement. It is positive. It enhances skills. Criticism focuses on the negative and reinforces negative tapes in the mind of the person being coached. (5) Anne needs to understand that good coaches keep their instructions simple. A good coach is not simplistic but is able to make it look easy and explain the changed behavior in such a way that the person being coached sees it as uncomplicated. (6) Anne, as coach, must seek to coach in the right place and at the right time. Good coaching occurs when the parties are uninterrupted. It is a private time between the coach and the player. The more private the time, the more effective the instruction. (7) Anne needs to be specific. Each act of coaching needs to focus directly on a specific act. Generalities add to confusion. By "chunking," Anne helps the player (teacher) improve one step at a time. (8) Anne needs to seek a balance between her positive affirmations of what each faculty member is doing right and constructive statements that suggest how each faculty member can be more effective. Again, these comments are most effective when done privately. And (9), Anne must be empathetic. An empathetic coach understands how difficult change can be for some members. They remember times in their lives when they had to learn new skills. By empathizing, Anne gains the confidence of her players (faculty) in this change process.

ASSESSING CHANGE

Since change involves doing things differently, Anne needs to assess its impact. Assessment needs to focus on individuals and the organization's structure. Since change is a complex process, assessment should begin immediately upon implementing the change and include descriptive data leading to the change. Assessment is both intermittent and long-term. It is ongoing and constructive. It enables Anne and her faculty to course-correct their initiatives before they become hampered by "sunk costs." When we refer to "sunk costs," we are referring to the commitment made to a project and then the unwillingness to let go of that commitment because of the emotional and physical resources previously spent to bolster the project even when the outcomes are negative. In this sense, the final product of change is unknown. The change product that the faculty developed is a guidepost that captures faculty focus. Anne should enlist the assistance of her faculty in developing an ongoing plan of assessment. The assessment should follow these steps:

STEP 1: PROVIDE DESCRIPTIVE DATA IN ASSESSMENT INFORMATION

Descriptive information assists Anne in assessing the change process and in determining if targeted end results are being met. Before Anne begins the assessment process, she needs to have a set of benchmarks by which progress is measured. These benchmarks are predetermined by her steering committee and progress toward them is shared with the entire faculty. In developing benchmarks, Anne can begin by describing the reason(s) why the change was initiated; the needs of the organization and its people that were not being met prior to the change; the rationale, goals, and objectives of the change; a summary of the discussions, minutes of meetings, and other deliberations such as recommendations made by focus groups; and a description of the process used to develop the change. Anne can include a calendar of events leading to the implementation of the change.

Step 2: Examine Targets and Choose Data-Collection Instruments

After identifying the needs of the organization and developing targeted goals for the change to help meet the needs, Anne needs to determine what types of data to collect to help track the course of change. In the end, after the master schedule is changed, Anne needs to determine if the dropout rate is decreasing and if teachers are developing new strategies to work with at-risk students. It is obvious that Anne will need to keep track of the number of dropouts. She could also track attendance, number of detentions, and involvement in extracurricular activities. Interviews with at-risk students could also be used as a means to collect qualitative data on the schedule change. Qualitative data provides descriptively rich insights about the targeted audience.

REFLECTION

How frequently are changes assessed within your organization? If they are not assessed, why aren't they assessed?

Anne should also measure the impact of the change on her teachers by utilizing surveys that she develops and commercial instruments that measure such areas as climate and satisfaction. Anne could also plan a series of informal observations to see what types of activities are occurring during the homeroom period.

STEP 3: CHECK THE IMPACT OF THE CHANGE ON THE STRUCTURE OF THE SCHOOL

Anne needs to cross-check results against intended goals of the change with the overall goals and objectives of the institution. Anne needs to determine if other areas of the organization were impacted. This information is used to help Anne make modifications and develop contingency plans as Latrobe implements the new master schedule.

STEP 4: EXAMINE AND ASSESS MORE THAN THE PERCEIVED END

Anne needs to assess the personnel used, the resources, and the types of training and/or staff development utilized within the plan. For example, Anne might have manipulated the schedule to have those she considers the "best" teachers as homeroom teachers. At this point, Anne and her faculty need to assess if this schedule is the "answer." Perhaps this change process opens the possibility of new paradigms that need to be explored. Anne should respond favorably to faculty readiness to continued growth.

STEP 5: EXAMINE DATA INDEPENDENTLY

The data needs to be focused on accurately assessing the outcome of the intended change. All relevant data needs to be collected. This relevant data is neither positive nor negative. It is accurate. It reflects reality. When it reflects reality it is positive, because it allows the organization to take steps that insure the quality of its product to its constituents. Anne moves toward, data not away from data.

STEP 6: SHARE RESULTS

Anne needs to develop a plan to disseminate information. She should consider developing a report every quarter or at the end of the first and second semesters. Anne should distribute results to teachers, parents, the central administration, the board of education, and the larger community. Anne could share the results in a variety of modes. A written plan is one way of sharing results. Other modes include media interviews, presentations at the homes of parents, meetings with small groups of faculty and students, and a visual, multimedia presentation.

PULLING IT TOGETHER

FIELD BASED PROJECTS

1. Interview your immediate supervisor. Ask him or her what changes the school is facing in the future. Ask the supervisor to elaborate on how he or she plans to manage one of these changes.
   - What steps will the supervisor take to involve people in the process from beginning to end?
   - What challenges will the school face as a result of this change?
   - What types of support will the school give to teachers as they work with the change?
   - What types of resources will the district give to the school?
   - How will the supervisor monitor the change?
   - Based on what you discover through this interview, what modifications in the planned change will you suggest to your supervisor?

2. Select three members of your school community and ask them to give reasons why they fear change. Embrace change? Problems they see with the way change is implemented and evaluated? From these perspectives, go back and examine the modifications you would offer to your supervisor in Field Based Project One. Have your modifications changed as a result of speaking with your colleagues? What modifications would you now make to this plan?

3. Arrange to speak with a board of education member. Ask this member to identify one major policy change about to

be enacted by the board. Use the following to guide your discussion:

♦   How did the board of education come to the decision to enact this change? What part of the school or district (or both) will be most affected by this change?

♦   If this is a policy that affects teachers and principals, find out if the teachers and principals were involved in its development.

♦   Ask what types of data were collected and how this data was analyzed.

♦   Who was involved in this analysis?

♦   How will the board announce the change? Enact the change? Support the change process? What are the similarities and differences between the change process in your building and at the board of education (district level)? Is this change a first or second order change? Why?

FIELD BASED ANALYSIS

1. Choose a change that you have experienced in a school system. How did you and others learn that the change was going to occur? How did you react to the way in which you learned about the change? How did your supervisor involve people in the change process? At what point were you involved in the change? If you had been the supervisor, how would you have introduced the change? What obstacles did the supervisor encounter in the early stages of the change? In later stages? Identify the obstacles that were related to people. What people skills either enhanced or detracted from the change process? Identify the obstacles that were related to the organizational structure. From this list, what organizational obstacles could have been eliminated? How could these obstacles have been eliminated? What supervisory skills could the supervisor have utilized to eliminate these obstacles? What obstacles (personnel and organizational) is the school still facing as a result of the change?

2. For the change you chose in Field Based Analysis One, examine the same change, but now analyze this change with regard to the concepts of first and second order change. In your opinion, was the change a first or second order change? What leads you to this conclusion?

3. Interview your superintendent. Ask the superintendent how she or he operationalized a change that is being mandated by the board of education. What steps does the superintendent need to take at the central administration office? With building-level administrators? How does the superintendent monitor change that has been initiated this way? What inherent obstacles does the superintendent face in monitoring and evaluating change? What types of follow-up activities are involved in this type of change.

IF YOU WERE ANNE LESTER...

How would you utilize the counseling staff to assist in presenting the data about the dropout problem during the faculty meeting?

How could you have better readied the faculty for the change in the master schedule?

How would you deal with "the old guard" faculty who oppose the change in the master schedule?

What would you do to reduce the fear and apprehension about the change in the master schedule?

What steps would you take to ready Latrobe High School for the change in the master schedule?

Would it be difficult for you to challenge marginal performance?

Would you challenge a subordinate whose performance is marginal? If yes, why?

What steps would you take to provide ongoing support to teachers after the change in the master schedule takes place?

How would you open communications (both formal and informal) at Latrobe High School?

How would you handle the perception by some teachers that you are a puppet of the superintendent and the board of education?

What types of information would you want to collect and then share with teachers, parents, and the superintendent after the change in the master schedule occurs?

What types of training and activities would you want to develop to help teachers work better with average students?

RESOURCES FOR SUPERVISORS

BOOKS

Belasco, J.A. *Teaching the Elephant to Dance: The Manager's Guide to Empowering Change.* New York: Crown Publishers (1990).

Calabrese, R.L., Short G., & Zepeda, S.J., *Hands-on Leadership Tools for Principals.* Larchmont, NY: Eye On Education (1996).

Fullan, M., *The New Meaning of Educational Change.* New York: Teachers College Press (1991).

Hall, G.E., & Hord, S.M., *Change in Schools: Facilitating the Process.* Albany: State University of New York Press (1987).

WEB SITE

http://www.ascd.org (Home page for the Association for Supervision and Curriculum Development).

5

SUCCESSFUL ORGANIZATIONAL STRATEGIES FOR SUPERVISORS

BUILDING BLOCKS

Roles
Beliefs
Values
Motivators

INTRODUCTION

As you read this chapter, continually reflect upon the organizational structure in your workplace. While examining the organizational structure, ask yourself how you, as the supervisor, fit in the organizational structure. What unique skills and abilities do you have to work within the system? What types of leadership skills are needed to build alliances to accomplish organizational goals? And, how can you organize the people in your building to achieve these goals?

Understanding the organizational structure in your school setting is a complex task. It is the supervisor's challenge to understand the people who comprise the school community, the processes that drive fundamental issues, how decisions are made, and how committees are formed.

Supervisors need to consider the strengths they bring to the position, their style of leadership, and how they communicate with the various groups that comprise the school community. As you read this chapter, examine the concepts presented. Reflect on the actions of the person in the supervision situation. Ask yourself, "What should the supervisor do?" and, "How should the supervisor do it differently?"

SUPERVISION SITUATION

Roberta Langley, a 10-year building-level principal at Larusa Elementary School, was transferred to Compton Elementary School by her superintendent. Roberta was flattered by the superintendent's vote of confidence in her abilities as a building administrator. Roberta was apprehensive about this transfer because Compton was in chaos. The former principal had been at Compton for 17 years. There were rumors that he had been asked to take an early retirement. Among the problems that plagued Compton were the continuing decline in achievement test scores, teacher turnover and requests for transfers, low parent and community support, and poor teacher participation in optional district staff development programs. Roberta's superintendent told her that "Compton used to be a great place for teachers and kids. I want to be proud of this school, and I know you can restore confidence in this school."

REFLECTION

Is Roberta at a disadvantage because she is the superintendent's choice? What obstacle do you foresee her facing with the Compton faculty and staff?

Although Roberta is a supervisor with experience in this district, she now has a new role to play. Her previous experience will be of help, but she is in uncharted waters. In reality, she is a new supervisor in this building and needs to determine how she fits into the school's overall structure as well as that of the community.

DEVELOP A PROFILE OF THE SCHOOL AND ITS PEOPLE

To understand the organizational structure, Roberta needs to find out about the people, programs, policies, and procedures that drive Compton Elementary School. The identification of the organizational structure begins with the examination of documents that reveal the history, mission, and goals of the organization. Nearly every organization has an existing mission statement and set of goals and objectives. This type of document review will assist Roberta in understanding the context and values of Compton and the community. There are a wide variety of materials available to Roberta. They include materials related to community values, school ethics policies and behaviors, programs that support the achievement of goals, operational committees, routes of power and influence, and operational policies such as attendance and discipline.

Frequently, the data that Roberta needs to examine are "hidden" in school documents. Roberta needs to examine the faculty handbook, student handbook, principal's newsletters to parents and community, end-of-the year reports, minutes of committee meetings, accreditation association and state reports, and job descriptions. Additionally, Roberta can review official correspondence between the former principal and community members, parents, students, and faculty. These documents provide a context as she prepares to assume her new role.

The mission statements of the school and district act as an interpretive lens. Roberta needs to allow these documents to be the basis for her understanding of the organization's actions—if the mission statements actively drive organization decisions. If the mission statements do not drive the organization's actions, then Roberta must discover the reasons for this "nonconnection." The amount of potential data to review may overwhelm Roberta. Adding to her sense of information overload is the qualitative data that Roberta will gain from conversations with assistant principals, deans, lead teachers, and department chairs. This information will give her emotional insights and a historical perspective about the organization and its structure.

FILTERING UNNEEDED INFORMATION

Roberta can be overwhelmed with unnecessary information. She needs to discern useful from superfluous information. Essential information is targeted to her needs. For example, Roberta has been given a charge by the superintendent to "recreate Compton." Roberta needs to prioritize the issues she faces and then target the information that helps to explain those issues. When Roberta targets information, she controls its flow. In effect, she manages the information so that it provides documentation of the source of the problems and lays the groundwork for potential solutions. The key point is that information is important when it is useful. Information becomes superfluous when it adds to the clutter. Roberta, as an effective supervisor, manages her time more effectively by controlling the type and amount of information that she has to review.

CONSTRUCT A FLOW CHART OF THE ORGANIZATION

Roberta can make sense of the organization by developing an organizational flow chart. A flow chart highlights the various roles, policies, and personnel. To chart the school's organizational structure, construct a flow chart that shows (1) the positions (e.g., the administrative team: principal, assistant principals, deans, department chairs), support personnel (e.g., custodial, secretary, cafeteria), and who reports to these people; (2) the programs that these people are responsible for (e.g., guidance department, activities, sports, student support teams, special education, attendance, discipline); (3) the relationships of these people and programs to the district (e.g., who at the district office regulates and coordinates these efforts, such as the director of gifted and talented, the athletic director, the assistant superintendent for curriculum and instruction), and the personnel (teachers and staff and their areas of expertise) in the building who coordinate, sponsor, and organize programs. Figure 5.1 is an example of a flow chart.

This flow chart illustrates the positions, programs, personnel, and the relationships between the building and district. Roberta can determine where she fits into the organizational structure. This type of charting experience will lead Roberta to documents that describe positions (job descriptions), and programs (e.g., at-risk program), and profiles of the people who coordinate and/or work within these areas (coaches, assistant principals, support staff).

Through this process, Roberta will discover the range of experience of employees (e.g., number of years in the position) and the significant faculty and staff contributions. By scouting these documents, Roberta is able to analyze the hierarchical structures by subject area, grade level, departments, and programs. Moreover, she will gain critical insights about organizational programs or areas that need bolstering or moni-

Figure 5.1. Organizational Flow Chart

Position	Programs	Relationships	Personnel & Expertise
English Department Chair	English Department, Writing Center, English tutors, related co-curricular (e.g., school newspaper, yearbook, literary journal, speech and drama club)	District Language Arts Coordinator	English teachers, moderators (e.g., school newspaper), Writing Center Coordinator
Assistant Principal	Student services (guidance counselors, nurse, social worker, psychologist), attendance office	Principal, district student services coordinator	Guidance counselor, attendance secretary

toring. As Roberta uses this process, she gains a comprehensive view of her school's internal and external organization.

REFLECTION

Why would it be critical for a supervisor to learn the history of school policy? Do you understand the history of key policies at your worksite? What do you think you would discover?

FORMAL AND INFORMAL ORGANIZATION STRUCTURES

Formal groups such as unions, teacher groups, and community organizations have an impact on the school. In this sense, these groups help form the school's organizational identity. Roberta should examine the ways these groups interact regarding form, function, and outcome by asking these questions: What role do these groups play in the day-to-day operations of the school? What teachers are involved in these groups? How do teachers feel about these groups? What activities and/or services do these groups provide for students, parents, and teachers? What operating procedures, goals, and objectives are common to these groups? What role does the principal play within these groups? How does the principal communicate with these groups? And, what is the history of these groups?

These groups impact the ways in which Roberta interacts and performs her duties. Consider this example. In the *Compton Teacher's Handbook and Contract*, it states that, "The administration must give 48 hours notification of a formal classroom observation." What does this mean to Roberta? Does this mean that she cannot do "pop-in" visits because of the "48-hour" negotiated agreement between the district and the teachers? Roberta needs to know how the union has interpreted this agreement. If the union has successfully grieved her predecessor regarding this issue, then Roberta will need to collaborate with the union to find common ground regarding the interpretation of this policy.

TIP

Create open supervisory communication channels.

Staff development committees and Sunshine Clubs are examples of *informal groups*. By examining these groups and their function, Roberta develops a feeling for how they work and contribute to communication among teachers and staff. One school with a Sunshine Club asks teachers and administrators to donate money once a year to defray costs for flowers for a sick teacher, baby shower gifts, and other human relations items. By examining the actions of these groups, Roberta can gather information related to the faculty's sense of community. When there is a strong culture of community, the morale is high, working conditions are positive, and faculty and staff have a feeling of "togetherness."

With this information, Roberta can reflect on how and where she fits into the organization. Supervisors monitor and provide leadership in the development of these programs and the people who work within their structures.

DETERMINE HOW AND WHERE YOU FIT IN THE ORGANIZATION'S STRUCTURE

As Roberta becomes aware of the complexities of the organizational structure, she can define her role, identify professional and personal boundaries, and accurately identify the school's ethos. Roberta can increase her awareness of the school's ethos by understanding past decision-making procedures and processes. She needs to know the role teachers play in making critical decisions. From this information, Roberta can forecast how teachers will respond to empowering initiatives.

Roberta needs to examine formal and informal communication channels. *Formal* channels include memos, faculty meetings, and committee meeting summaries and minutes. *Informal* channels include communication in the faculty lounge, hallways, playground, parking lot, and at social activities such as holiday celebrations and special events that bring people together.

Roberta invested critical time examining the organizational structure at Compton Elementary. She now needs to reflect on her prior supervisory experiences and look deep within herself to examine her strengths and weaknesses. By doing this, Roberta will take stock of her personal strengths and potential derailers before beginning her new position. Roberta can do this by following this six-step process. She can also use this process to help her faculty and staff to determine their strengths and potential derailers.

STEP 1: LIST MAJOR ACCOMPLISHMENTS AND DETERMINE

- How she was able to accomplish these tasks.
- The organization skills that allowed her to accomplish these goals.
- The people skills that allowed her to get people moving toward the accomplishment of these tasks.
- The stumbling blocks she encountered.
- Her responses to these stumbling blocks.

STEP 2: REVIEW SUMMATIVE EVALUATION REPORTS HER PAST SUPERORDINATE DEVELOPED

- What were acknowledged as strengths and potential derailers?
- What goals were set to address potential derailers?
- What types of advice and/or insights were given by the superordinate?

STEP 3: SEEK FACULTY AND STAFF INPUT ABOUT EFFORTS

Some supervisors receive feedback from their subordinates. Typically, this feedback is in the form of a survey assessment similar to the instrument in Figure 5.2.

FIGURE 5.2. SUPERVISORY ASSESSMENT INSTRUMENT

MEMO

From: Roberta Langley
RE: Supervisory Assessment Instrument

Dear Colleagues,

As a new supervisor, it's important to me to assess my work with teachers and staff members. Therefore, I would appreciate it if you would complete the survey and return it to my secretary. **Do not sign your name!**

In your opinion, what can I do to become a more effective supervisor? Be honest. I can only grow when I receive honest feedback from those who know me best. You are those people.

STEP 4: SEEK FEEDBACK FROM A MENTOR

If Roberta had a mentor who was familiar with her work setting (such as a fellow supervisor in the same district), she could ask for specific feedback about her strengths and potential derailers.

STEP 5: LOOK FOR COMMON THEMES

Common themes can be discovered by examining like data that emerges from what superordinate and subordinates reveal about you. After finding the common themes, formulate goals or targets for change. Whatever method used, Roberta should develop change-related goals.

STEP 6: REVIEW GOALS PERIODICALLY TO CHECK ON PROGRESS

This process can assist Roberta in assessing critical supervisory areas such as *Human Relations Skills, Communication Skills,* and *Organization and Planning Skills.* Human relations skills are essential for Roberta to succeed. Roberta realizes that her actions, words, and deeds are tied to building trust and positive human relations. If she has good human relations skills, she will be able to mobilize members of the organization.

Communication skills allow Roberta to understand her faculty and staff. An effective supervisor is able to listen, gather information, and know what to say when. There are no "mixed messages" sent by Roberta's words, actions, and deeds. Communication messages are consistent. She communicates comfortably with confidence with the *formal* and *informal* groups of her school.

Organization and planning skills keep Roberta focused on meeting the unit's objectives. These skills include delegation, empowerment, and pacing. When Roberta releases personal control, she increases the productivity of her faculty and staff by openly displaying trust in their abilities and fostering ownership. Delegating, according to Douglas and Douglas, "involves a dilemma: We must keep what we want to give up—the responsibility; and we must give up what we want to keep—the authority."[1] There is an art to effectively delegating work, according to Douglass and Douglass, who provide these guidelines:

- ♦ Think and plan first.
- ♦ Clarify the job responsibilities.
- ♦ Select the right person.

---

[1] Merrill E. Douglass and Donna N. Douglass, *Time Management for Teams.* New York: American Management Association (1992), p. 190.

- ♦ Decide on authority levels.
- ♦ Set appropriate controls.
- ♦ Maintain a motivating environment.
- ♦ Hold the person you choose accountable.[2]

REFLECTION

Why is it important for a supervisor to know his or her strengths and potential derailers?

When Roberta empowers her faculty and staff to make decisions, she demonstrates trust in their ability to competently complete a task while unsupervised. Razik and Swanson believe that "Empowerment is the ability of leaders through an active and creative exchange of power to encourage followers to achieve a vision and realize goals."[3]

Roberta understands the concept of pacing when she avoids making hasty decisions and putting unnecessary pressure on faculty and unit members. Pacing takes into account the professional, psychological, and personal needs of staff and faculty. Roberta needs to understand the fine balance between "pushing" and "demanding." She needs to understand that constant pushing conforms to the "law of diminishing returns." When she operates under the concept of pacing, she allows for rest stops, plateauing, and personal restoration.

Daniel Jennings believes that "leadership is a 'people' activity...not a problem-solving activity."[4] Looking at Jennings' notion that leadership is a people activity, one must think about the leaders they have known and what people skills

---

[2] *Ibid.*

[3] Taher A. Razik and Austin D. Swanson, *The Fundamental Concepts of Educational Leadership and Management.* Englewood Cliffs, NJ: Prentice-Hall (1995), p. 59.

[4] Daniel Jennings, *Effective Supervision: Frontline Management for the 90s.* St. Paul, MN: West Publishing (1993), p. 201.

they had which enabled them to emerge as leaders and sustain their positions. Roberta's mentor, Josephine Greenmax, encouraged her to go back to college and get the training needed to become an administrator. Roberta listed the traits that made Josephine an effective leader. These traits included self-assurance, humor, credibility, courage, openness and flexibility, enthusiasm, and integrity.

Josephine was self-assured. She was confident with words and actions. Confidence comes in part through being comfortable with knowing who you are and what you represent. Josephine had been a teacher for 15 years before becoming a supervisor. As a supervisor, she never lost sight of the teacher's role. There were very few awkward interactions with teachers, parents, students, and staff members, because Josephine was honest.

Josephine used humor to diffuse potentially volatile situations. Best of all, Josephine was able to laugh at herself. She once said, "Learn not to take yourself too seriously."

Josephine had credibility. Those who worked for Josephine trusted that she could accomplish what she said she could accomplish. Without credibility, a supervisor is able to exert little leadership, motivation, or influence with his or her teachers and staff.

Josephine could take a stand and make decisions that were unpopular when she was convinced of their authenticity. She was not continually changing her mind. Her faculty was impressed with her courage. Roberta remembered the time that Josephine stood up to the school board and would not recommend their handpicked choice for her school's basketball team.

Josephine was open to the life flow of the organization, its needs, and its people. She recognized that organizations are continually changing. She was open to change and the sense of discovery it offered. If Roberta is not open or flexible, her school will become stagnant, and her staff and faculty will become complacent.

Josephine championed the individual and his or her contributions. Achievements were celebrated publicly and without hesitation. She used failed attempts at change as learning opportunities. At all times, Josephine honored risk taking. Risk taking became a value at Josephine's school.

Josephine was ethical and equitable to teachers, staff, and students. She was a person of integrity. She did not play favorites, give special privileges, or make undue exceptions in the way she treated people.

REFLECTION

Have you ever had a supervisor whom you could use as a model in the way Roberta relied on Josephine? What made this person a model for you?

As a supervisor, Roberta needs to understand herself and her motivations. She needs to know how she reacts and interacts, how she responds to issues, and how her actions, beliefs, and decisions impact her faculty, staff, and students. She needs to know what she believes about students, teaching, and learning. By understanding these issues, Roberta can communicate her beliefs to teachers and staff members.

IDENTIFY PERSONAL MOTIVATORS

Personal motivators include a wide variety of variables that Roberta brings to the position. For example, she may feel a need to lead, reform, or nurture people. Maslow's hierarchy of lower and higher needs are worth considering as Roberta reflects on personal motivators:

> **Survival needs**: the basic needs of the moment.
>
> **Security needs**: predictability of life-style, family, and group membership.
>
> **Belonging needs**: acceptance—people want to be with you.
>
> **Esteem needs**: recognition by others as having special abilities and valuable characteristics.

Need for knowledge: knowing how to do things.

Need for understanding: being able to make meaning from events; knowledge of systems and processes.

Aesthetic needs: appreciation for order and balance; a sense of beauty in and love for all.[5]

Not only does Roberta have these basic needs, but her subordinates have these same needs. Daresh and Playko believe that "motivation is one of the most important and challenging supervisory responsibilities undertaken in schools or any other organization."[6]

Roberta should determine her essential needs. To do this, she must consider her prior teaching, administrative achievements, and experiences; current situation, motivation, views of power, leadership, ambition; and personal expectations. Insight into these areas is gained by reflecting on life as world experiences. For example, Roberta discovered that students who ate lunch during the fourth period lost 5 minutes of instruction every day. Five minutes a day may appear insignificant. However, calculated over time, 5 minutes a day can cause a loss of 18 hours of instruction throughout the year —almost a full week of school! She was concerned. She discovered that the teachers were not aware of the impact of this schedule on student time for learning. Nor were the teachers particularly worried.

Roberta wanted to increase instructional time. Yet, she realized if she moved too quickly she would lose ground with her subordinates by not recognizing their needs. On the other hand, if she does not motivate teachers to examine the issue,

---

[5] N.L. Gage and David C. Berliner, *Educational Psychology*. Boston: Houghton Mifflin (1988), p. 146.

[6] John C. Daresh and Marsha A. Playko, *Supervision as a Proactive Process: Concepts and Cases*. IL: Waveland Press (1995), p. 146.

she will discard her values. Roberta checked with the union and their agreement, with the superintendent, and with other district principals. Other building-level principals indicated that their schedules were balanced; hence, a single group of students were not missing instructional time so teachers could have additional preparation time. The superintendent gave preliminary support to Roberta to change the schedule. Roberta realized that the master schedule was an issue. Before she acted, she needed critical information from her teachers.

Roberta reflected on her motivation. She realized that several central beliefs drove her organizational decisions. First, she believed that parents have a right to hold the school accountable. Second, she believed that people need to be involved in making decisions that affect their lives. And third, she believed that students had a right to a quality education. These beliefs shaped her view of the organization's functions.

FIND A MATCH BETWEEN WHAT MOTIVATES YOU VERSUS WHAT MOTIVATES YOUR STAFF

Just as Roberta's primary motivation was her belief in accountability, there were teachers who were motivated by time, that is, more time to prepare for teaching, which, they believed, provided improved instruction. Each person is motivated either *internally* or *externally* by subconscious forces. Potkay and Allen believe that "the aim of any motive is identified by the particular satisfaction brought about by a person's actions, such as having a positive emotional relationship with another person (affiliation motive) or having control over the behavior of another person (power motive)."[7] Roberta's decision to work with her subordinates indicates that she is motivated by affiliation, the need to have positive relationships with members of her unit. However, externally Roberta is motivated by her superordinate's desire for her to bolster the aca-

---

[7] Charles R. Potkay and Ben P. Allen, *Personality: Theory, Research, and Application.* Monterey, CA: Brooks/Cole Publishing (1986), p. 347.

demic program and falling test scores. If Roberta had changed the master schedule without staff consultation, she would have been motivated by power to control the actions and behaviors of her unit's members.

INTERNAL MOTIVATORS

D.C. McClelland identified three motivators: achievement, power, and affiliation.

ACHIEVEMENT

Supervisors who are motivated by achievement are interested in success; they take pride in accomplishing goals with distinction, and they are competitive. Achievement-oriented supervisors have a standard of excellence that they hold as a marker of achievement. This type of supervisor is a long-distance runner by remaining committed to project completion.

POWER

Supervisors who are motivated by power are preoccupied with control and exact precision over activities and the people involved. Roberta's influence is associated with power. Power has five classifications. *Reward power*, where rewards are used to motivate subordinates. *Coercive power*, where punishment is used as a means of motivation. *Legitimate power*, where the power-user is viewed as credible and uses this credibility to influence people. *Referent power*, where the power user is respected by subordinates. Respect creates an identification between the power user and subordinates. It is this identification that motivates subordinates to work with the power-user to achieve goals. And *expert power*, where the power user is perceived as an expert. This perception of expertise motivates subordinates because they have confidence in the person with expert power.[8]

REFLECTION

What motivates you? Are you motivated by power, affiliation, or some other need? What do you think motivates your current supervisor?

AFFILIATION

Supervisors who are motivated by collaborative needs value human relations, open communication, and lasting relationships with subordinates. Frederick Herzberg, a noted psychologist, developed a theory of motivation that delineates the satisfaction workers derive from *internal* and *external* rewards. Herzberg classified rewards into two categories: *Hygiene Factors* (external factors that might motivate subordinates) and *Motivators* (internal factors that motivate peak performance in subordinates). *Hygiene Factors* include such items as job security, salary and fringe benefits, and the organizational climate and physical conditions of the work environment. Hygiene factors are critical and add to the quality of the work environment, but Herzberg believed that these factors alone do not motivate people to achieve their full potential. Herzberg believed that the *internal motivators* such as achievement, professional and personal growth, added responsibility, and recognition motivated subordinates to achieve greater personal and organizational results.

For example, teachers are motivated to earn a master's degree to receive both internal and external rewards. Consider some possible *internal* rewards of getting a master's degree: (1) lifelong learning; (2) accomplishment of a goal; (3) higher status in the community as a "better"-educated teacher; (4) recognition as a subject-matter specialist. Some possible

---

[8] Razik and Swanson, *op. cit.*, p. 44.

external rewards to getting a master's degree are (1) pay raise; (2) rise in status; (3) subject-matter specialist. There are, at times, places of intersection between internal and external rewards.

Roberta and her staff are both motivated to give students the best possible education. However, a conflict may occur if Roberta's accountability beliefs drive her to change the schedule without considering her teachers' need to have more time to prepare for instruction or eat lunch. Roberta's decision to work with her teachers makes it clear that she believes in the importance of working with teachers. This is a balance that Roberta needs to maintain. It is her responsibility to discover common ground associated with her belief system and that of her teachers.

Roberta needs to place her beliefs and motivations into action; otherwise, teachers will believe that she lacks integrity. Teachers desire to know and understand Roberta's expectations. Roberta should spend time with her faculty discussing beliefs, attitudes, and values. The time that she spends with her faculty will build trust. Trust is the cornerstone in the building of relationships and bolstering morale and positive work environments.

DETERMINING VALUES

There are competing values in a school: Roberta's values, school cultural values, community values, district values, and teacher and staff member values. It is relatively easy to identify these values by examining the organization's symbols and myths. The values a school embraces are readily evident. It is more difficult to determine individual values. The difficulty arises from the inability of people to identify their values.

TIP

Bring an outside consultant in to facilitate the value discovery process. This allows you, as supervisor, to participate with your unit.

Value identification is critical for Roberta. Roberta needs to recognize her values and communicate those values by words, deeds, and actions to teachers, faculty members, students, and parents. Roberta is the person who represents the organization to teachers, district administration, students, parents, and the community. Her values are viewed by the community as the school's values.

Consider the example of Jill Strong, a fifth-grade teacher at Compton. Jill has, in a sense, become an institution at Compton. Colleagues, administrators, and community members often seek Jill's opinion because of her reputation. When Jill speaks, faculty and staff members listen. This underscores the values that are embedded in the people who work in organizations. This is why it is essential for Roberta to discover the values of the members of her school. By listening, Roberta discovers individual and organizational values. Roberta can determine if the individual's values are aligned with organizational values and if his or her values are aligned with those of the members of the organization and with the organization. This alignment process will assist Roberta in understanding organizational life, areas of conflict, and areas of collaboration.

Examining the values, beliefs, and attitudes within an organization is a time-consuming process. *Time* for Roberta is a premium. There are many concrete tasks and deadlines to meet. Time pressures may force Roberta to go through the motions of identifying her values. Periodically, Roberta should review her behavior to determine if (1) there have been changes and shifts in her values, beliefs, and attitudes; (2) alignment of the organization regarding goals and objectives is needed; (3) changes need to be made to better meet organizational goals and objectives. The results of reflection and the action chosen will make Roberta more effective.

MAPPING STRATEGY

Our discussions have centered on the exploration of values, beliefs, and attitudes, and how these factors motivate Roberta. Now our attention shifts to linking these items to the school's organizational structure and the people who comprise the school.

To make the link between personal and organizational values and beliefs, Roberta needs to go through the process of alignment. Roberta can use the following guidelines to chart the similarities and differences she has with her organization. First, Roberta should identify the values, beliefs, and attitudes that motivate her. Second, Roberta should identify the values and beliefs of her superordinate and subordinates. And third, Roberta should identify positive or negative relationships between her beliefs, attitudes, and motivations and those of her organization. Once Roberta has aligned the beliefs, attitudes, and motivations of the faculty and administration at Compton, she can turn her focus to the essential tools that she needs for success.

TOOL ONE: EXPANDING THE VISION

The word "tools" is deceptive. If Roberta considers tools in a narrow sense she may view classroom supervision as a clinical supervisory model where there is a *preobservation conference*, an *observation*, and a *postobservation conference*. However, when we expand the definition of "tools," we find that Roberta's tools include the policies of the organization, the diagnostic and prescriptive interactions between Roberta and others, and any activity undertaken by Roberta that promotes the organization and its members.

REFLECTION

Does your current supervisor have a narrow or broad perspective of the supervisory role? What would you do in that situation?

TOOL TWO: EXPLORING ORGANIZATIONAL POLICIES THAT DRIVE SUPERVISORY PRACTICES AND PROCESSES

For Roberta to understand the supervision of teachers within the organization, she needs to explore district policies and procedures, including *formal* and *informal supervisory procedures*. Roberta needs to understand the district's procedures regarding formal and informal supervisory procedures. She needs to examine the policies that drive formal and informal supervision of teachers and certified and noncertified staff.

Formal supervisory procedures identify types of observations, number of required visits; frequency of visits; yearly deadlines that must be met; and procedures that reflect differences in supervisory practices for beginning teachers, tenured teachers, and teachers on plans of improvements (remediation). *Formal observations* follow a specified format such as a preobservation conference, observation, and a postobservation conference. Best practice recommends that documentation of some type be shared with the teacher. *Informal observations* are made by supervisors for a shorter period of class time. They are unannounced, and typically, little documentation follows the observation.

Some contracts and policies will be silent about these supervisory practices; however, others will specify the conditions such as number and frequency of these types of classroom visitations. Roberta needs to examine the language to determine if the district follows any type of cycle for the differences in supervisory practices for novice and veteran teachers. For veteran teachers (tenured or continuing contracts), some districts follow an every-other-year cycle of formal supervision and evaluation. Other districts do not require yearly formal observations of tenured or continuing contract teachers. For novice teachers, many districts provide guidelines that are specific about the nature of classroom observations, the procedures to be followed, and the frequency of observations.

Roberta must follow prescribed policies—exactly; otherwise, grievances most likely will be filed, which may lead to bad feelings and even to litigation. When grievances are filed, morale suffers and Roberta's impact and credibility are jeopardized.

TOOL THREE: DEVELOPING A SUPERVISORY PLAN TO CARRY OUT DISTRICT POLICIES AND PROCEDURES

Roberta needs to plan for supervision by providing mandated supervisory practices. Roberta should start by identifying the teachers in her building who must be observed and/or evaluated during the current evaluation cycle. Once Roberta has collected these data, she should determine what she values about teaching and learning. These values should focus on these specific areas: materials, classroom management, teacher behavior during class, student learning, and the organization of class for effective instruction. Roberta assists her teachers in attaching values to each area by connecting discussion of the area to values that the teacher holds.

Roberta needs to examine the informal organizational norms that drive supervisory practices in her district. Roberta's first step is to assess past supervisory practices. She can assess past supervisory practices by conducting formal and informal focus groups with teachers to discover their beliefs regarding past practices. The focus groups provide Roberta with valuable information regarding teacher attitudes toward formal and informal supervision. The data she collects will help her understand the history and emotions connected with supervision in her building. Roberta does not have to live with the history, but she does have to understand its influence if she hopes to shape existing practices.

TOOL FOUR: DEVELOPING A SUPERVISORY PLAN

Roberta needs to chart how she is going to achieve the number of formal and informal visitations. To develop this schedule and tracking system, she should use a computer-driven spreadsheet. The spreadsheet includes all tasks (goal setting, pre- and postobservation conferences) that are explicitly stated in the policy.

Roberta should not wait until the end of the year to do formal observations. This is a key flaw of many school supervisors. If Roberta waits to the end of the year to work with teachers, she will undermine quality supervisory practices. This process does not promote the growth that comes from a well-organized value-driven system. A well-organized, value-driven system allows Roberta to do follow-up work with teachers after formal observations. As a result, Roberta can provide additional assistance to teachers and staff.

TOOL FIVE: COMMUNICATING THIS PLAN TO THE FACULTY AND STAFF

Each year Roberta needs to review district policy regarding supervision and evaluation of her faculty and staff. If Roberta reviews the policy with union officials, her school administrative team, and other key players, she can facilitate a common understanding related to the goals and objectives of supervision and reaffirm the supervision values that drive this process.

TOOL SIX: EXAMINING THE IMPACT OF SUPERVISION ON STAFF AND ITS RELATIONSHIP TO CURRENT PRACTICES AND INITIATIVES

Roberta needs to link supervision of faculty and certified staff to other schoolwide goals and school improvement initiatives. Roberta is responsible for examining the organization's effectiveness through attainment of these goals. There is an interrelationship among these goals. Efforts in one area impact all other areas. For example, Roberta, after having observed all the third-grade math teachers, reviewed the curriculum guide. She found that several teachers refused to use an inquiry through the use of manipulatives-teaching strategy. Roberta consulted with the district curriculum coordinator and discovered that only two of the seven teachers had been trained in this method. The majority of teachers were unprepared to achieve the district's instructional goals. The lack of teacher training caused student confusion and parent complaints and affected teacher morale. The kind of problem faced by Roberta can be eliminated by linking the results of supervision to the overall needs of the building. Roberta can use the following seven-step process to create the necessary linkages.

REFLECTION

How effective is the supervisory process at your current worksite? Does your supervisor have a supervision plan mapped out to follow? What would you do differently?

STEP 1: ROBERTA SHOULD EXAMINE CURRENT INSTRUCTIONAL GOALS TO DETERMINE THE PROJECTED RESULTS

If current goals have been achieved, Roberta needs to lead her teachers through a process of developing new goals or aligning goals more specific to the organization and its needs. If the goals have not been achieved, Roberta needs to determine if the goals are still valid or the reasons for the faculty's inability to meet the goals.

STEP 2: ROBERTA NEEDS TO CONSULT WITH TEACHERS

She has to encourage teachers to openly discuss their fears and concerns regarding the supervision process. By providing time for these critical discussions, Roberta assures her faculty of her commitment to this process. This is an appropriate use of staff development time.

STEP 3: ROBERTA NEEDS TO ALLOW TEACHERS TO BE PART OF THE SOLUTION

Diagnosis and prescription must occur through a dialectic that includes all pertinent parties to the supervisory process. When Roberta creates this dialectic she will witness the generation of a collaboratively generated synthesis. All faculty will be on the same page regarding the purpose and process of supervision.

STEP 4: ROBERTA NEEDS TO ACQUIRE ADDITIONAL RESOURCES FOR TEACHER AND ORGANIZATIONAL NEEDS

Roberta should coordinate the resources of the building with those of the district. When Roberta uses her influence to divert district resources to the instructional process, she demonstrates to her faculty that she is an effective leader who collaboratively recognizes the instructional limitations of faculty and is able to provide the means to apply prescriptive remedies.

STEP 5: ROBERTA SHOULD MONITOR THE PROGRESS AND IMPACT OF STAFF DEVELOPMENT ACTIVITIES

Roberta needs to continually solicit feedback from teachers regarding the effectiveness of staff development activities. The feedback she receives should include as much objective data as possible. Items such as lesson plans, test results, and videotaped lessons are excellent sources of data.

STEP 6: ROBERTA NEEDS TO COMMUNICATE INITIATIVES TO THE ENTIRE FACULTY

Informed teachers will help eliminate misinterpretation of Roberta's role in supporting the efforts of teachers. Rumors spread through an organization when information is limited. When Roberta diffuses information throughout the faculty there is little room for rumor generation.

STEP 7: ROBERTA NEEDS TO REINFORCE AND AFFIRM
THE EFFORTS OF TEACHERS

When Roberta affirms excellent practices, it should be public and contribute to the building of the organization's ethos. Public affirmation reinforces the values that Roberta and the faculty have embraced. It sends a strong message to faculty that excellent performance is recognized and rewarded.

Daniel Jennings noted that "supervisors need to create an atmosphere that encourages, supports, and sustains improvement."[9] The development of this atmosphere occurs gradually. It occurs best when supervisors know their people. Roberta can develop positive relationships with the people in the organization by being visible in the school during passing periods, by informally and formally observing classrooms, and by affirming the strengths of the people in the organization.

Roberta is committed to professional growth and model learning behaviors when she participates with her faculty as an equal in staff development activities and other learning opportunities. Her presence and active interaction signals the importance of this activity to her faculty.

TOOL SEVEN: VISUALIZING SUPERVISION IN A BROAD PERSPECTIVE

Roberta has a specific focus of responsibility. Yet, within that focus are myriad tasks. If Roberta's vision is too narrow, some tasks may be neglected. Examine Roberta's responsibilities as principal. Many programs have an impact on the organization of the school and its instructional programs. Some areas that need supervision include attendance, discipline, health counseling, and social services. In addition to people, programs and processes need to be evaluated. These include curricular offerings, the master schedule, before- and after-school activities and programs, parent organizations, and the

---

[9] Jennings, *op. cit.*, p. 205.

budget. Roberta must monitor the effectiveness of each of these programs. She can monitor the effectiveness of each by understanding the program and then determining if goals and objectives are being met. Roberta cannot limit the extent of her vision.

TOOL EIGHT: BUILDING ALLIANCES TO ACCOMPLISH GOALS

Roberta works with and through people. People are her school's primary resources. Roberta can be more effective when she recognizes that her organization exists to serve the needs of people. Compton Elementary School is only a mythical shell which provides a context in which people gather together to work for common ends.

Working together to meet mutually conceived goals is an ideal that is difficult to achieve. It takes considerable effort to approach this ideal because of the complexities inherent in each human personality. Consider Roberta's situation at Compton Elementary. Roberta is not new to the district. In fact, she has been a principal for 10 years. Roberta is a successful leader who has developed good working relationships. These relationships took time to develop. Moreover, Roberta, like any other person in a leadership role, has detractors in her building. These detractors have not supported her decisions; they often act as obstructionists as she tries to improve the organization. Roberta will always have detractors. It is her task to minimize their influence on the impact of faculty.

The astute supervisor realizes that the people who comprise the school community—teachers, staff, parents, and students—can either move or sabotage a system. Much of Roberta's efforts must be directed to developing a sense of community to facilitate this movement in a positive direction. There are several strategies that Roberta can apply to minimize disruption and to move toward the ideal.

STRATEGY ONE: ROBERTA NEEDS TO KNOW HER AUDIENCE

This is a beginning point for Roberta. She needs to identify the strengths and weaknesses of each member of her organization.

STRATEGY TWO: ROBERTA NEEDS TO IDENTIFY STRENGTHS AND POTENTIAL DERAILERS IN HER FACULTY AND STAFF

Joe Batten's book, *Tough-Minded Leadership*, stresses the importance of identifying the strengths of subordinates. Batten believes that supervisors need to "expand people, not compress them, to build on their strengths, not focus on their weaknesses."[10] Roberta can rely on documents such as past performance reports, perceptions of other superordinates, or even her own perceptions over time as a way of identifying strengths and weaknesses. Or Roberta can ask subordinates to *identify* their own strengths. A three-step process based on the work of Batten can be used by Roberta to identify strengths and potential derailers.

STEP 1: WORK WITH SMALL GROUPS OF TEACHERS

Ask teachers to independently self-identify five strengths they bring to the unit. These strengths may be personal or professional.

STEP 2: IDENTIFY EACH OTHER'S PERCEIVED STRENGTHS

Ask members to identify two or three strengths they believe each of the other members possesses. Have people share these insights about each other.

---

[10] Joe D. Batten, *Tough-Minded Leadership*. New York: American Management Association (1990), p. 53.

STEP 3: CREATE AN OPENNESS SO PEOPLE CAN REVEAL THEIR OWN PERCEPTIONS OF SELF

Encourage each participant to reveal self-perceptions about his or her own strengths by disclosing the self-identified strengths in step 1. As participants reveal self-perceptions a sense of trust is generated.

Roberta can use this information to build rapport with unit members. She can, as Batten indicates, "realize the limitless and barely tapped potential of joint human effort." From this exercise, Roberta gains insight into the needs of her faculty and staff. This is especially true if Roberta, like Batten, believes a weakness is an absence of a strength. If Roberta is interested in establishing *collaborative* relationships with her subordinates, then this approach will help. On the other hand, if Roberta has a need to dominate subordinates, then information gathered from the self-identification of strengths minus weaknesses will be of little assistance. From Roberta's decision not to change the master schedule without first motivating and challenging her teachers to face issues, we can assume that Roberta is more concerned with affiliative ways of working with faculty and staff.

TOOL NINE: MAPPING TASKS AND PROJECTS

Roberta needs to build collaborative teams as she manages units, people who comprise these units, and the tasks that need to completed. Roberta can facilitate this undertaking by mapping tasks and projects. Effective mapping begins with setting priorities. Some tasks take priority over others. Roberta needs to examine the organizational goals and determine which tasks take priority. She may use the talents of her faculty by establishing an advisory council. The advisory council can assist Roberta in setting priorities, mapping strategies, and assessing outcomes. To set priorities, we recommend that Roberta do a **SWOT** analysis. **SWOT** is an acronym for "strengths, weaknesses, opportunities, and threats." It is a commonly used business strategy. This is an excellent team-building activity. Roberta can lead her team in setting priorities by having them:

Step 1: Do a SWOT analysis by having groups list

- Strengths of the organization (e.g., supportive parent group)
- Weaknesses (e.g., students are scoring lower on state achievement tests)
- Opportunities (e.g., increased student performance will allow us to be named a "high performing" school by the state association)
- Threats (e.g., continued decline in test scores will result in state sanctions)

REFLECTION

What would a SWOT analysis reveal about your current worksite? What would be its strengths, weaknesses, opportunities, and threats?

Step 2: Generate short- and long-term goals.

Step 3: Identify specific programs or their development to attain goals.

Step 4: Assign responsibility.

Step 5: Identify evaluation target dates.

Step 6: Review progress.

Step 7: Go back to Step 1.

Roberta can identify the tasks involved in project completion. Complex projects have multiple tasks. Roberta should determine the nature of each task—daily, weekly, monthly, quarterly, or yearly. Some tasks can be classified as one-time or repeating. Moreover, these tasks should be viewed in the context of time (e.g., short-term, long-term, and ongoing). Once the nature of the tasks has been identified, goals need to be established.

Roberta should enlist the support of subordinates. Unit members can make valuable contributions to the unit. By involving unit members, Roberta provides the conditions that generate commitment. Roberta can generate commitment and build a community of workers committed to each other. Roberta generates support by establishing a need, illustrating the benefits to the unit through member's support of activities, and by encouraging subordinates to get involved with activities.

Roberta should facilitate the work of subordinates. Teachers are busy. They have high demands placed upon them. Roberta can facilitate the work of her teachers by taking care of as much of the detail work as possible. She can clear the path for teachers and their work. She takes the lead by clearing the way for members to work during meeting times by providing the needed resources to complete tasks and projects and by following up on items and issues that surface in meetings.

Roberta should monitor task completion. She should check task progress by involving unit members in monitoring their own progress. Supervisors often report to a superordinate. Roberta should report the progress of tasks and activities to her superordinate. By monitoring task progress, Roberta can report tasks or aspects of tasks that have been completed, tasks still under construction, obstacles that have prevented the unit from completing tasks and activities, deadlines (projected) for task completion, and resources needed to complete tasks.

Roberta should regroup efforts when necessary. Through participation in the mapping of tasks and activities and monitoring completion progress, Roberta can spot detours. This type of early and ongoing involvement assists Roberta in taking a proactive approach to regrouping efforts. She can always refer to the SWOT steps as a means of regrouping team efforts.

Roberta should organize subordinates to achieve common goals. Organizing people to achieve common goals depends on Roberta's willingness to hear the voice of the members of the organization. One way to hear the voice of subordinates is to create cooperative teams. While forming teams, Roberta needs to consider faculty representation. Faculty representation includes a representative base of the faculty. It's easy for Roberta to fall into the trap of relying on those who have become personally close. Continual dependency on these members divides the faculty, builds cliques, and limits the distribution of rewards. Roberta can be more effective if she operates with a inclusion policy.

Roberta should establish processes and procedures for selecting team members. Her process should be fair and equitable by encouraging faculty to nominate and elect members. Subordinates who self-select to serve on teams and/or committees are usually committed to the tasks involved in achieving the committee's goals. However, Roberta should ask, "Can the people committed to these tasks work well together?" Roberta needs to be aware of the synergy that is likely to develop on the team. One way to predict the potential synergy is to "test" the team for personality preferences, operating styles, or decision-making styles. Roberta might want to discover, for example, team members' decision-making styles. Roberta could use the Calabrese *Decision Making Inventory* (DMI)[11] to profile the types of decision makers found within the team. The DMI is a 140-item, multiple-choice instrument situated within the context of a complex case study. The DMI assesses the quality of decision making in 13 subcategories (curriculum, student discipline, parents, teachers, parents, problem-solving, leadership, policy, ethics, gangs, cultural diversity, and organization). When used as a tool, the DMI can:

  ♦   Diagnose the quality of decisions made by the team.
  ♦   Screen team members.
  ♦   Assist supervisors to facilitate the work and processes the team uses to complete tasks.

---

[11] Raymond L. Calabrese, *Decision Making Inventory*. San Antonio, TX: Decision-Making Systems (1994).

- ♦ Give direction in identifying team training needs.
- ♦ Assist teams in learning how to come to consensus over tough issues and decisions that need to be made within the context of the organization.

TIP

Use the *Decision Making Inventory* to develop a personal plan of growth for people interested in becoming school supervisors.

Roberta should consider the scope of the activities her team will address. In addition to considering the strengths of team members, Roberta needs to ascertain whether team members have the time to commit to the work of a team. Competing interests (cocurricular activities before and after school, personal commitments such as graduate school, and professional responsibilities such as involvement in organizations and districtwide activities) might prevent a unit member from assuming another activity. There is an adage, "Ask the busiest person to do something, and it will get done." This adage derails the composition of a committee if team members are extended to the point of nonproductivity.

These essential tools are critical for Roberta. They allow her to effectively guide her school on a day-to-day basis toward the accomplishment of the school's mission. Without organizational tools, the school is a rudderless ship adrift in the ocean. There may be much activity on board, but little headway is made against the ocean currents. By becoming versed in the organization tools suggested in this chapter, Roberta can apply them to her position at Compton for the benefit of the Compton school community.

PULLING IT TOGETHER

FIELD BASED PROJECTS

1. Choose a school other than the one in which you are employed. Secure a copy of the faculty handbook, district employee handbook, and a description of as many standing committees as possible. After obtaining and studying these documents, develop a flow chart in which you identify positions, programs, relationships, and the personnel who comprise the school community. Then interview the supervisors to review your initial analysis of constructing the positions, programs, relationships, and the personnel who comprise the school community. What positions, programs, relationships, and personnel did you omit in your analysis? This field based project simulates the struggle and frustration a new supervisor encounters while trying to develop an understanding of the complexities of an organization.

2. Interview your principal or immediate supervisor. Ask this supervisor how he or she learned about the organizational structure of the school during his or her first year. Ask specifically what steps they took to learn about the organization *before* the school year began and what steps they took to learn about the organization *during* the course of the year. Ask them to share how they would modify their approach if they were to assume a new position in a different school. Now review the information of this chapter.

3. Meet with a supervisor and teach this person about the SWOT process of identifying strengths, weaknesses, obstacles, and threats. Ask this supervisor to apply the SWOT process to a current situation the school is facing. If you work in this building, you might be tempted to enter into the application. Refrain from doing so, as the objective of this field-based project is to give you the opportunity to hear and see a supervisor model problem identification. Next, analyze and reflect upon applying the SWOT proc-

ess. If you are employed in this building, you will be able to analyze whether or not Roberta missed any critical aspects during this process.

FIELD BASED ANALYSIS

1. Construct a flow chart of your organization. Identify both formal and informal groups that comprise the school community. Examine the informal groups and answer these questions:

    ♦   What role do these groups play in the day-to-day operations of the school?
    ♦   What teachers are involved in these groups?
    ♦   How do teachers feel about these groups?
    ♦   What activities and/or services do these groups provide for students, parents, and teachers?
    ♦   What operating procedures, goals, and objectives are common to these groups?
    ♦   What role does the principal play within these groups?
    ♦   How does the principal communicate with these groups?
    ♦   What is the history of these groups?

    Are there any generalizations you can make regarding these informal groups? If you were to assume a supervisory position within your building, would there be any one or two informal groups that could exert influence over you in your new capacity? Elaborate.

2. Reflect upon your school and immediate supervisor. How does this person delegate? If you were recently delegated to accomplish a task for your supervisor, how did this supervisor:

    ♦   Clarify the specifications of the task?
    ♦   Assist you when you encountered problems?
    ♦   Monitor your work? Did you have to seek out assistance, or did your supervisor monitor your work closely enough to know when you needed assistance?

- Acknowledge your work? Publicly? Privately? Hold you accountable?
- Handle decisions that had to be made?
- Give you authority to make decisions, or were you required to bring information to this supervisor any time a decision had to be made?
- Support the decisions you made after having given you authority to make decisions?

Overall, what did you learn about delegation from those in subordinate and supervisory positions?

3. If you were to assume a supervisory position in 2 weeks, what would be the most important information for you to learn? What would be the most efficient way for you to learn this information? Based upon what you identify as "the most important" information to learn, construct and gather this information from within your organization.

IF YOU WERE ROBERTA LANGLEY...

How would you get to know the Compton teachers?

How would you address the apparent apathy of teachers, students, and parents?

Would you want to speak with the former principal?

How would you begin forming a team?

What would you want to communicate to the Compton teachers during the first faculty meeting?

Why would it be important for you to know the strengths and weaknesses of the teachers?

What would you do with the knowledge of subordinate's strengths and weaknesses?

How often would you want to get feedback about your performance from teachers? Superordinate?

How would you utilize teams in the building during your first year as principal?

How would you broach the topic of lost instructional time?

How would you handle a grievance from a teacher who felt your attempts to change the schedule were harassment?

How would you handle the teacher's apparent lack of concern that students were losing instructional time?

How would you respond if your teachers refused to discuss the change in the master schedule?

How would you communicate the results of your discussions with the superintendent?

What would you do at the end of the year if your beliefs were at odds with the overall Compton community?

What would you do if your teachers kept their classroom doors locked, and you could not easily gain access to their classrooms for the purposes of observing them teach?

How would you motivate your teachers to develop a set of common goals?

RESOURCES FOR SUPERVISORS

BOOKS

Calabrese, R.L., Short, G. & Zepeda, S.J., *Hands-on Leadership Tools for Principals.* Larchmont, NY: Eye on Education (1996).

Rosen, R.H. with Brown, P.B., *Leading People: Transforming Business from the Inside Out.* New York: Penguin Books (1996).

WEB SITE

http://inet.ed.gov/ (Home page for the U.S. Department of Education).

6

SUCCESSFUL TEAM BUILDING FOR SUPERVISORS

BUILDING BLOCKS

Selection
Relationships
Disrupters
Support

INTRODUCTION

The work of organizations is best accomplished by the collective efforts of people working collaboratively toward common ends. This "team effort" links the aspirations of the people within the organization to the those of the organization. In a collective sense, the school and its community are a team if they work together to accomplish goals and objectives. However, within the structure of a school, the communal team is comprised of smaller units contributing to the cause and purposes of the larger unit.

Teams can accomplish much in the appropriate environment. Effective supervisors know the importance of teams, their capacity to accomplish great results, and the dynamics that can be harnessed by teamwork and play. Great teams do not assemble by chance. Teams are formed and developed to accomplish specific goals, perform certain tasks, or review certain aspects of an organization. Effective teams are given authority to make recommendations, develop action plans, draft policies and procedures. In the end, they have a positive and significant impact on their organization. However, dysfunctional teams harm the organization regardless of the environment. Dysfunctional teams do not work well, they are unfocused about their purpose and function, and they breed discord within the organization. This type of team does more harm than good. Consequently, supervisors need to have the skills to form and nurture effective teams. By learning the skills of team development and maintenance, supervisors boost morale, foster collegiality, and enhance the school's educational, psychological, and physical environment. As you read this chapter, examine the various concepts presented. Reflect on the actions of the person in the supervision situation. Ask yourself if this person used the building blocks of effective team building, and how the building blocks mentioned in the chapter may have been more effectively utilized. Constantly ask yourself, "What should the supervisor do?" and, "How should the supervisor do it differently?"

SUPERVISORY SITUATION

Mike Sorelli, principal of Milton Elementary School, was faced with developing a 5-year plan to improve the educational achievement of the students at Milton Elementary School. Mike believed that this task could be met by involving teachers in the planning. However, Mike found no evidence that his staff had previous experience working as a team on a large project. In the past, Mike formed committees to work on textbook adoption, staff development, and the discipline issues. These efforts were not tied to long-term planning, nor were they highly complex. Their short duration did not build the collaborative team spirit that Mike felt was essential for this project. Mike was fortunate because there was strong faculty commitment to work together. He was also a realist and knew that he would have to spend a great deal of time and energy forming and shaping this team. Mike's first step in forming this long-term team was to present the idea to his newly formed advisory committee.

REFLECTION

What teams exist in your organization? How effective are these teams? How does the staff view the administration's support of the teams in your school?

Mike's advisory committee was formed as the result of a new state requirement mandating "site-based" committees. Mike's advisory committee had functioned well since its inception. However, they were lukewarm to his idea. The advisory committee did not understand why Mike wanted to form a new committee. As one member said, "We are the site-based committee; this should be our task." Mike tried to reassure the advisory committee that he was not replacing them, but was encouraging a greater sense of inclusion among the entire faculty. There was more discussion, but it was clear to Mike that he was not going to get the full support of his advisory committee. He felt that this team was split and that he had caused the split. He wondered how he could have handled this issue differently.

FORMING EFFECTIVE TEAMS

Mike experienced initial success at forming an effective team at Milton. However, he was unaware of the underlying dynamics that are essential in maintaining a functional team. He was unaware that wanting to form a team and knowing how to form an effective team are different. Mike often works with a variety of teams established to perform a specific function or achieve a goal. Some teams are long-standing and stay together an extended period of time, with its membership rotating. Other teams are short-term and disperse after achieving their objectives. Regardless of the type of team, Mike needs to know how to form effective teams. Francis and Young defined a team as "an energetic group of people who are committed to achieving common objectives, who work well together and enjoy doing so, and who produce high quality results."[1] This definition serves as a solid foundation for the work Mike Sorelli needs to accomplish in developing an effective team.

TIP

Create teams only when they are essential.

---

[1] Dave Francis and Don Young, *Improving Work Groups: A Practical Manual for Team Building.* San Diego, CA: University Associates (1979), p. 8.

HAVE THE ENDS IN MIND WHEN CREATING A TEAM

Mike must know what he needs his teams to accomplish. High performance teams, according to Larson and LaFasto, have a "clear understanding of the goal to be achieved and a belief that the goal embodies a worthwhile or important result."[2] This knowledge can assist Mike in identifying the people to involve in a specified task. The team Mike Sorelli wants to form will be charged with crafting and overseeing the school's 5-year plan. Mike wants this team to develop a focus for the faculty and students. To unify the efforts of the faculty at addressing weaknesses and acknowledging strengths, Mike needs a team to examine a variety of areas: student attendance, demographics, and achievement on standardized test scores. Mike chose these areas as targets because the state department of education issued a policy stating these areas are to be used to evaluate schools. Mike was making the same error with his new group that he made with his advisory group—he was setting the team's direction without team input. Mike's lack of trust was creating problems. Before Mike can initiate the process of forming and nurturing a functional team, he has to recognize the paradigm shift that is occurring in democratic institutions. No longer are people content to allow one person to dictate direction and work conditions. There is a strong need to participate in all phases of organizational decision-making. Mike is no longer the sole arbiter of decision making, policy setting, vision, mission, or direction. As the new democratic-driven workplace paradigm continues to evolve, Mike has to evolve to keep pace with these new demands. Mike must move away from the director toward the facilitator component. He also has to let go of the innate administrative heresy of not trusting employees to one of trusting the experience of the employees to drive decision making that is in the best

---

[2] Carl E. Larson and Frank M. LaFasto, *Teamwork: What Must Go Right/What Can Go Wrong.* Newbury Park, CA: Sage Publications (1989), p. 27.

interests of the group. Once Mike makes a commitment to embrace the role of facilitator and to trust his colleagues, he can effectively build and nurture functional teams.

REFLECTION

Are the teams at your school aware of their essential purpose? Do the members of these teams relate to the team's central purpose?

SELECTING TEAM MEMBERS

Once Mike has determined the general work to be accomplished by the team, he has to select team members. There are a variety of ways of forming teams. Teams can be formed by requesting volunteers, vote of staff, or personal request based on the strengths that the prospective member brings to the team. We discussed the strengths analysis in the previous chapter. We believe each of these methods is appropriate for specific contexts. For example, in highly volatile issues, requesting volunteers may be important because it allows those with a vested emotional interest to be part of the group. In this case, we recommend that any time the volunteer method is used, the balance of special interests be protected. The vote of staff is an important method when the members of the committee represent the entire staff. Mike's advisory committee should be chosen by a vote of the staff. The third method, selecting team members based on strengths, is used when targeting specific organizational objectives where the time limit and the group's objective are clearly identified. Being aware of the context is critical in team formation. Some contexts for Mike to consider when selecting team members include:

+ The work of the team: goals, objectives, tasks, and projects that occupy the team's efforts.
+ The types of expertise and experience needed to accomplish the team's work.

♦ Interest level—members of the faculty who have an emotional interest in the project.
♦ Special interest groups—clusters of people who are committed to this work.

To utilize the strengths and talents of his people, Mike needs to encourage involvement. He generates enthusiasm for work by making connections between teamwork and professional development. He shows the linkages to his faculty between new professional skills such as group processing techniques and classroom instruction. Mike can also point out how involvement on teams bolsters school cohesiveness by developing networks of people who have a vested interest in the school's success.

Mike may be inclined to choose team members who consistently follow through with assigned tasks. If he consistently follows this path, he might be perceived as having a "chosen" clique. His faculty may begin to view these cliques as power decision-making groups who serve Mike's best interests. If Mike follows this route, he will fail to develop team-building skills in faculty members and will create low morale, contribute to burnout, and generate a sense of divisiveness. Awareness of how groups are formed and the importance of inclusion eliminates this trap. As Mike becomes more aware of the pitfalls, he realizes that the selection process is critical. Once all members agree to serve, Mike introduces the committee to the school community.

DEVELOPING EFFECTIVE TEAMS

Mike builds effective teams through *creating a team identity*. To develop a strong team, Mike needs to exhibit behaviors and attitudes that support the building of a positive team identity. Team members need to be able to identify with the team, each other, and the team's tasks. Within the team setting, Mike should create an environment where team members explore meanings, craft new ways of approaching issues, and experiment with the implementation of ideas. For working relationships to develop which form the basis of teamwork, Mike needs to exhibit actions, deeds, and words that boost the self-esteem of each team member and the esteem of the team as a whole. High positive esteem is essential to success. Mike needs to consider the quality of care he provides to promote professional and personal pride in the members of teams and the work that they accomplish.

REFLECTION

How effective is your current supervisor at creating team identity? What would you do differently?

Mike creates a successful team by *supporting and modeling positive team behaviors.* The success of a team is dependent upon Mike's efforts and attitudes. When Mike models and supports positive team-player behaviors through feedback, empathy, and confidentiality, he builds a sense of "family" among members. This sense of family reinforces the commitment that each member makes toward the others.

Mike creates a successful team by valuing team members. Team members need to feel valued and supported in their efforts. It is our belief that the value supervisors place on team members drives their work and determines the success of the team. It is this value that transcends difficulties in the completion of teamwork.

DIRECTING TEAM EFFORTS

Mike's team will be more effective and gain confidence when he provides continuous support. Mike provides support through a variety of means including managing time, controlling the scope of information, building support at the macro level, increasing team member commitment, continuously clarifying the team's mission, and reviewing team history.[3]

Mike effectively manages the team's time when he aids in the prioritization of the issues that his team faces. It is Mike's responsibility to make sure that his team does not overextend its scope. It is better for the team to limit its vision and succeed than try to embrace an overly complex task and fail. Here, Mike has to create a balance between the time available to the team and the breadth of the project. Mike can increase the complexity of the project undertaken by the team if he can provide release time for its members.

A second way in which Mike provides support is through the control of the scope of the information that his team has to consider. Information is useful only in the sense that it is directly applicable to the task. Information that is not directly applicable may be interesting, but it takes away from the focus of the team—accomplishing its mission. It also confuses those who have to integrate numerous sources of information.

A third way in which Mike provides support is to build support at the macro level. Mike is the public spokesperson for the team's activities. He constantly interacts individually and in groups, in formal and informal settings, supporting the team's endeavors. He shares appropriate information and gauges the reaction to the information. Mike engages in a continuous dialogue with all groups who are affected by his team's work. Mike takes risks by being the point person for the team. Yet his willingness to risk public criticism serves as a buffer for members of his team.

A fourth way in which Mike provides support is his working to increase team members' commitment to the team's project. Mike increases commitment by asking for a public commitment from each member as the task progresses. "Joe,

---

[3] *See* Glenn Hallam, *The Adventures of Team Fantastic: A Practical Guide for Team Leaders and Members.* Greensboro, NC: Center for Creative Leadership (1996). It is an excellent source of additional ideas regarding the work of teams.

are you committed to what we have developed to date?" Joe's affirmation in front of his peers increases Joe's commitment. The team's commitment is also enhanced by Mike's willingness to give credit for the team's success to the team members. Public recognition of each member's efforts deepens the level of the member's commitment. Mike must refrain from taking personal credit for team efforts. If the team is successful, Mike will receive abundant credit.

A fifth way in which Mike provides support is by continuously clarifying the team's mission. The team must be periodically reminded of why it exists and its purpose in functioning. One way Mike can accomplish this task is to review the team's goals at fixed times and ask for an open assessment as to how these goals are being met. In an earlier chapter, we spoke of "benchmarking." Benchmarking is an important task for team leaders. It is a way of keeping the team focused.

REFLECTION

Think of a task assigned to a team at your school. What benchmarks were set to measure progress towards identified goals? If benchmarks were not established, why weren't they established? What benchmarks would you set?

A sixth way in which Mike provides support is to continuously review team history with team members. Each meeting contributes to the history of the team. Mike needs to remind the team members of where they started, obstacles they've overcome, successes they've had, and the journey that remains. Mike's effort to create a history generates conditions where members see the value of personal and collective contributions to this history. A sense of history binds one to the organization.

MANAGING TEAM DYNAMICS

To a certain extent, the team dynamics chart the team's journey. Mike needs to understand his team's dynamics through observation and analyzation. Mike increases his level of understanding by examining his team's characteristics to explain the ethos that it is likely to develop. Some characteristics that should be considered are the members' experience and background, the age of team members, the members' professional affiliations, the member's education, the members' relationships with other teachers, administrators, and the system, and the members' attitudes towards students, parents, and the community.

DEVELOPING EFFECTIVE GROUP HUMAN RELATIONS

The way Mike Sorelli interacts with team members at this first meeting is critical for the future success of the team's work. Team members will model their interactions with one another by observing Mike's communication style and facilitation approach. To this extent, the messages Mike sends during this first meeting will determine whether the group will be functional or dysfunctional.

During the first meeting, Mike establishes the ground rules. These ground rules work well in a variety of settings.

GROUND RULES FOR EFFECTIVE GROUPS

♦ *Create a safe environment.* Groups cannot function when members do not feel safe. Mike can create a safe environment by stating that (a) each person has a right to express him- or herself completely without interruption; (b) each person has a right to his or her opinion without fearing criticism; (c) ideas are addressed, not people; and (d) each person addresses the group through "I" statements rather than the attacking "you" statements. For example, a person may say, "I think that the concept we heard has some serious flaws." This is more effective than stating, "You're wrong if you think that will work!"

♦ *Appoint a facilitator.* Groups cannot function without a facilitator who understands how to involve group members. Without an adequate facilitator, strong members dominate discussion. Quiet members become passive participants.

♦ *Set time limits for discussion.* Some members want to dominate conversation. They are not conscious of the length of time that they occupy center stage. The facilitator should invoke this ground rule whenever the time limit in the ground rules is exceeded.

♦ *Agree on how you will agree.* As part of the ground rules, the group has to recognize whether agreements will be made through consensus or majority vote. Consensus needs to be defined if the group chooses to operate with this model. If the group chooses to operate with a majority vote, it needs to decide what type of majority vote. Will it be a simple majority, a two-thirds majority, or some other combination?

♦ *Understand the parameters of the authority of the group.* Clearly, the group needs to understand the limits to their authority. It is unfair to the group to give them the perception of unlimited authority and then to withdraw that authority at a later date. Be clear, accurate, and make sure that the group's authority is fully understood by all.

♦ *Agree on what is to be kept inside the group and what is to be shared outside the group at the closure of each meeting.* This is an area of trust that will either sustain or destroy a group. If a group is willing to safeguard discussions and only share agreed-on information, then the group will grow in personal commitment. Most failures in this area occur, not because of the lack of human integrity, but because of the uncertainty of what information is to be kept secure and what is to be shared. In general, secure information includes personal comments, personnel considerations, projected alternatives, and interpersonal conflicts among team members. Information to be shared includes decisions that are made, agreed-on progress statements, and minutes reflecting the agenda and responses to the agenda.

Once these ground rules are understood, Mike can let team members become acquainted with one another by encouraging people to introduce themselves and share their backgrounds and strengths. Wood, Killian, McQuarrie, and Thompson believe team members need to know each other before they can form as a well-functioning team because "it is difficult for people who know so little about their faculty members to trust them, to understand why they react as they do, or to recognize the different strengths among people within the school community."[4] Getting to "know each other" is a slow process even in organizations where people have worked closely together for years. Group work requires a form of intimacy that is missing in the typical organizational structure. As a facilitator, Mike must recognize that each member of the group brings a set of experiences that drive his or her perspective to the work of the team. Often, these perspectives are hidden because the team member is unsure of the response he or she will get to his or her perspectives. If Mike is a skillful facilitator and nurtures a safe environment, the members of the group will grow to "know each other."

---

[4] Fred Wood, Joyce Killian, Frank McQuarrie, and Steven Thompson, *How to Organize a School-Based Staff Development Program.* Alexandria, VA: Association for Supervision and Curriculum Development (1993), p. 4.

BUILDING THE FOUNDATION FOR FUNCTIONING GROUPS

To conduct a productive first meeting, Mike needs to do preliminary work such as highlighting issues, providing tentative timelines, and mapping basic phases of major projects. By having a clear idea of goals and timelines, team members can clarify their roles. Mike does his preliminary work by meeting individually with each team member. He uses this meeting to seek to understand the perspective that the team member brings to the group. He does not try to form the perspective. He honors the team member by informing them that their perspective is important and that it needs to be heard by the group.

PLAYING TOGETHER

Now that Mike Sorelli has assembled his team, set ground rules, and finished his preliminary work, he needs to focus on encouraging members to play well together. Teams typically work through such tasks as defining and understanding issues, initiating activities to reach the targeted objectives, and engaging in discussions. Teams have the capacity for derailment if the supervisor does not focus on creating an environment that promotes healthy relationships. Mike can keep team members moving forward with their work and play to accomplish goals if he knows how and when to intervene, how to keep the team focused, and how to generate agreements. Francis and Young believe that teams go through four stages of team development[5]:

THE TESTING STAGE

The testing stage is an awkward stage for team members. As teams initially form, members are unsure of their role and its relationship to the goals and objectives of the work. Team members may or may not be familiar with one another because they may be separated by grade level, subject matter, teaching schedule, or communication network. Team members may not have conceptualized the macro picture; instead they may have a myopic vision.

THE INFIGHTING STAGE

The infighting stage is the stage where members "jockey" their roles and functions, establishing positions of power and influence. Effective supervisors assist team members to assume and sustain equal roles. Within the structure of the team, leaders and followers emerge. Mike needs to keep a balance by encouraging all members to play.

THE GETTING ORGANIZED STAGE

The getting organized stage is characterized by members organizing themselves to accomplish the work of the team because of a personal commitment to the work and to other members of the team. During this stage, team members are concerned with developing skills for getting along with one another, establishing communication channels, and beginning the work of the team. They have moved away from a limited vision of their teaching to a more global conceptualization of the team's work.

---

[5] Francis and Young, *op. cit.*, pp. 8–11.

THE MATURE CLOSENESS STAGE

The mature closeness stage is characterized by respect between and among members. Camaraderie and good will open pathways for team members to support each other and their work. These pathways can be opened because team members have formed close relationships. They know each other's values and beliefs. They provide support and encouragement to each other. In high functioning teams, members experience a sense of interdependence by adapting a "sink or swim" attitude. In a sense, the team's work creates a bonding effect.

REFLECTION

Consider any teams in which you currently participate. What is their stage of development? Are they stuck at this stage?

EFFECTIVE MOVEMENT THROUGH THE STAGES OF TEAM DEVELOPMENT

Mike can facilitate the work of the team while keeping an eye on the unfolding dynamics between team members and their work by assuming a facilitative role. To accomplish this, Mike needs to focus on five key areas.

AREA ONE: OPEN INTERGROUP COMMUNICATIONS

Mike can ensure that all team members have the opportunity to share their beliefs and values. Initially, Mike can organize team members into small groups so interactions can be more open and direct. Forming small groups will assist later by preparing members to work on small-step tasks and projects associated with developing the 5-year plan.

AREA TWO: ENCOURAGE TEAM MEMBERS TO RESOLVE THEIR OWN PROBLEMS AND DISAGREEMENTS

Mike should refrain from intervening in conflicts among and between members as they identify their roles. Mike needs to provide a safe environment and assist team members in clarifying their roles as part of the struggle of learning how to interact in a team setting. He needs to intervene as a mediator rather than as a judge. When Mike mediates disagreements, he teaches the team members how to peacefully resolve disagreements.

AREA THREE: PROVIDE REFLECTION

Mike needs to act as a reflective agent to help the team analyze their work and interactions with one another. As a reflective agent Mike continually asks the group, "What if...?" He focuses on the potential consequences of actions and ties them to the emotions of the group. Asking, "How do you feel about this?" encourages an emotional reflective response from each group member.

AREA FOUR: DEVELOP COMMUNICATION CHANNELS FOR INTER- AND INTRATEAM COMMUNICATIONS

Teams need to interact with other aspects of the organization. Information needs to be multidirectional, flowing within the team and from the team to the rest of the organization. Mike needs to find ways to encourage feedback. Feedback from within and outside the team provides information which helps to determine whether or not goals are being met and to identify other needs that emerge.

AREA FIVE: CLARIFY TEAM BOUNDARIES

Teams work more efficiently if they know the boundaries of activity and authority. Mike should establish loose–tight boundaries, which include decision-making authority. Empowered teams feel invested in the cause, tasks, goals, and activities. Members are more likely to support the team efforts, publicly and privately, when boundaries have been clarified.

UNDERSTANDING THE TEAM PROCESS

This section deals with assisting the supervisor to understand the team process. Teams, as they develop, go through stages, changing over time to meet desired needs and goals. As Mike works with this new team, he examines the following stages to nurture the development of a functioning team.

Team processes occur in the *Conceptual Stage*. Mike should encourage team members to conceptualize their work by examining the *needs* and *goals* underlying the tasks and activities which bring the team together. From this conceptualization, an understanding of the unit's needs becomes clearer, and team members begin developing *clarity* of purpose.

Team processes occur in the *Task Orientation Stage*. Mike needs to lead team members into framing specific tasks. Once tasks have been formed, concrete steps can be taken to accomplish tasks, set timelines, establish priorities, and define roles. Mike's role is to act as a supportive facilitator clarifying task purpose and intent, leading the team through discussions and deliberations, and serving as a source of motivation. This last aspect is significant. High functioning teams have supervisors with superior motivational skills.

Team processes occur in the *Task Implementation Stage*. Mike guides team members in bringing to fruition their ideas by assisting them to reach desired outcomes. The task implementation stage is an important part of the team process; however, it is often neglected. There is a tendency for teams to "let down" once they perceive that they have completed their mission. We believe that when teams recognize that they have oversight responsibility for implementation and evaluation, their commitment to process endures and a "let down" is avoided.

THE SUPERVISOR AND THE TEAM—
THE RELATIONSHIP

There are four specific roles that Mike will assume with this team in developing the school's 5-year plan and school improvement plan. These roles include facilitation and record keeping, mediation, reflection, and motivation.

FACILITATION AND RECORD KEEPING

Mike can keep his team focused through effective facilitation of the group. Effective facilitation includes appropriate feedback to make sure that the group understands what a team member has said, gentle probing to help the member explain more fully what they intended to say, and continual monitoring of progress toward the group's ultimate goal. When Mike compiles all data, he filters out inessential information. Records can help Mike chronicle work, ideas, and problem-solving processes. These records will help Mike analyze how and why certain decisions were made. Recording progress also assists team members in focusing on the team's objectives. This documentation keeps the rest of the community informed of the team's work and serves as a marker of the team's success.

MEDIATION

Everyone in a team sees the world differently. When these views conflict they have the potential to be divisive. As a result, relationships become strained as members begin to place competing views on the table. Mike needs to be ready to mediate differences before they split the group into opposing camps.

Throughout the team process, people need to be able to disagree with one another, openly, and without fear. Moreover, Mike needs to be detached from the team's dynamics. A hasty intervention will stifle this necessary and healthy response as the team asks difficult questions, probes differing perspectives, and challenges the complex issues. Mediation means that Mike will not take sides. His main concern is in arriving at the best solution, not necessarily a compromise. Mediation takes time. However, the time invested in mediation will serve the group far better than a hastily negotiated peace.

Reflection

How receptive are you to feedback about your performance? How can your supervisor enhance the quality of feedback that is provided to you? Does your current team receive feedback from your supervisor?

Reflection

Team members will look to Mike for guidance regarding their ideas, innovations, or solutions. Mike needs to be ready to give feedback on the feasibility of their ideas and solutions. Feedback is different from judgment. When Mike provides feedback he assists the team member in a reflective examination of his or her ideas. When Mike judges an idea he opens or closes a door on the team member. Seasoned supervisors know that reflective feedback is the best option. It allows the team member to "work through" the complexities of the concept.

Motivation

Mike needs to provide encouragement and support to his team. The work involved in developing a 5-year plan is ongoing in nature; therefore, Mike will need to motivate his team. Teamwork is tedious. It is fraught with interpersonal conflict. It often moves without any seeming progress. Mike acts to encourage, to remind the members of their original vision, and to provide hope that their mission is possible. Mike needs to make sure that the team members stay focused. In effect, Mike does more encouraging through his actions and personal commitment to the team's mission than through exhortation.

INCREASING AWARENESS IN THE TEAM'S WORK

Mike needs to maintain open communication channels so the team can share information with the larger unit. Open lines of communication make it possible for his team to get feedback about their work. This feedback is especially critical for the teams at Milton since the faculty has little experience in the team process. Moreover, the primary outcome of the team's work will be a 5-year and school improvement plan.

To achieve open lines of communication between the team and the larger unit, Mike needs to assist the team in organizing information so that it can be presented to the entire faculty. Ironically, many people focus on the presentation of formal reports as the most important form of communication. However, Robert Waterman told the story of a consulting trip to Japan where the CEO of a large bank resisted the formal report for weeks and asked that the preparation team continue to meet. Finally, when the team made its presentation to the CEO, the CEO had heard all of the team's plans through the company's "grapevine." In effect, team members constantly talk to their colleagues whether or not they are team members.[6] Encouragement of this dialogue is critical. It allows the entire faculty to be "stress inoculated" to the work of the group. There are no surprises. This informal communication method provides an interactive response between the team and the larger faculty.

---

[6] Robert H. Waterman, *The Renewal Factor: How the Best Get and Keep the Competitive Edge*. New York: Bantam Books (1987).

TEAM DISRUPTION

By examining the dynamics of a team, Mike can pinpoint pressure points. Once pressure points are eliminated, teamwork can be enhanced. Team members can distract the team from accomplishing their goals. For example, a member of Mike's advisory committee may begin to disclose information about Mike's plans before Mike has formalized them. This disclosure creates a stressful environment for the faculty as they begin to place personal interpretations on Mike's potential actions. Although Mike has made no decision, team members can purposely sabotage his efforts.

There are a variety of disrupting behaviors including *control, criticism, complacency,* and *vacillation.* Subordinates who use excessive control over team members try to influence team decisions. Control is manifested through such tactics as monopolizing discussions and politicking before and after team meetings to influence the outcome. Mike should intervene by promoting openness to ideas and shared authority among team members. Mike may have to speak privately to the dominating member. If private coaching does not work, Mike will have to address the matter with the team. When he addresses the matter with the group, Mike asks them to discuss the issue of the disruption and seeks their advice on how to handle this type of disruption. In this way, Mike facilitates the discussion of the problem and refrains from judging the person or the issue.

Subordinates who use excessive criticism undermine the team's confidence. Criticism alienates members and reduces commitment. Mike does not want to eliminate criticism. It is healthy. However, Mike needs to find ways to make criticism constructive. We suggest that 10 minutes of every meeting be opened to criticism of the team's work. As a ground rule to this segment, we further suggest that personal criticisms not be allowed. Once personal criticism is allowed, issues are forgotten and individual members seek to protect their idealized images.

Subordinates who are complacent are not motivated to engage in team efforts. This sense of passivity seems to be generated by a lack of effort rather than as a means of undermining the group's efforts. The complacent team member may not trust the group, may have a physical problem, or may not have an interest in the issue. In any event, Mike needs to make an effort to understand the source of the member's complacency before it reaches a contagious stage.

Subordinates who vacillate often derail team members by causing them to revisit tasks and activities that have already been resolved. They waste time by seeking to renegotiate past agreements, review previous decisions, and act as if commitment was nonexistent. Mike needs to prevent this behavior by asking for public commitment to each decision and then recording that commitment in the team's minutes. In this way, Mike can refer to the minutes each time this strategy is employed by the disrupter.

REFLECTION

Consider the disrupters of the team process at your school. What strategies do they use to disrupt the team's progress?

We believe that disruptive behavior is best handled by proactive facilitation. Proactive facilitation focuses on positive outcomes. It looks for the good that comes out of any situation. Mike can use disruption to the good of the team. For example, let's assume that Robin Heasley, a member of the advisory committee, was the member who leaked the information about Mike's plan. At the next meeting Mike proactively responds to the group:

Mike: At our last meeting I mentioned the possible formation of an important faculty-led task force that will focus on instruction. No decision was made. Yet, word of the discussion reached the faculty and caused undue stress. I don't want to cause the faculty unnecessary stress. How should we handle our discussions in the future?

Robin: I mentioned it to some faculty members. However, I didn't know how they would respond. I think that our meetings should be open and that anything we say can be shared with the faculty.

Mike: Robin, please correct me if I paraphrase your statement incorrectly. Robin states that anything we say in here can be shared with others. How do you feel, Joan? (Mike then asks the opinions of each member of the group.)

Eventually, Robin sees that the members of the team don't want to share all that is said in the team meeting. Mike, acting proactively, asks the team to establish guidelines. He then asks for public commitment to those guidelines. Robin makes the public commitment. Mike has effectively dealt with this situation. Robin has been disarmed without being injured. Mike can even thank Robin for raising the issue.

HOW TO RECOGNIZE THE LIFE CYCLE OF A TEAM

The life cycle of a team depends, to a certain extent, on the team's work and composition and the needs of the organization. Some organizations require teams to work continuously. Consider Mike Sorelli's team. This team will focus on school improvement. This requires a continuous focus. The tasks associated with developing and implementing a 5-year plan can be achieved in a relatively short period of time. However, monitoring and evaluating occur over a longer time frame and require ongoing coordination and collaboration.

More importantly, teams are given birth, they have a life, and there is time for the team to die. The preparation for each of these stages of team life is important. We have spoken about the birth of the team, as well as the importance of insuring that the birth is healthy and has the opportunities to succeed. We have spoken about the maturing of the team. During the maturation process the team has to face and surmount challenges. It has to identify its mission. It has to develop strategies to achieve its mission. It has to take responsibility for the implementation of its initiatives. Similarly, the team has to be prepared to die. Dying is an important part of the team process. If the team is a functioning team, the dying will be more difficult. The members have bonded, they have survived by collectively facing obstacles, and they have grown more intimate with each other. They literally were a team that became a family. A dysfunctional team does not have this problem.

REFLECTION

Consider the teams currently active in your school. Where are they in their life cycle? Should they be buried?

Mike has to prepare the team for dying. He has to announce to the team, in advance, when their tasks are finished. He has to "celebrate" the team's death so that the team members have a closure to their efforts. He has to allow for a mourning period for the team before moving forward with another initiative which may involve members of the functional team. Mike's willingness to recognize this strong emotional need will further solidify his leadership, and it will add to the meaningfulness of team membership in his school.

Some teams have a kind of permanence in school organizations. The same concepts which we just mentioned apply to these teams. On permanent teams, it is the member who is born, matures, and dies in terms of membership. The rotation process provides for the cycle of members to take place so that there are members at every stage of team cycle. The procedures for rotating team members need to be formalized by procedure and policy. Policy makes transitions easier and eliminates awkwardness. When a member's term is up, make sure that this member leaves notes or any other items pertaining to projects or work that he or she is currently developing. New members can benefit from this type of information. Effective supervisors induct new members into the team. Induction processes shape behavior and expectations by explaining the ways in which the team functions, people interact and communicate, and the roles people play. The induction process allows the supervisor to provide a new team member with the team's history, future, myths, symbols, and vision.

ALIGNING TEAM GOALS WITH ORGANIZATIONAL GOALS

Mike is on the right track by incorporating the work of the mandated school improvement plan with the work of developing a long-term 5-year plan. The work of teams should complement the goals of the school. Teams and their work should be viewed as one way of achieving goals. For this to occur, Mike needs to align the work of teams with the purposes of the organization. He ensures that teams and their work achieve organizational goals through strategic planning. Strategic planning by the team allows the collaborative development of long-term plans, identification of the goals and objectives of the organization, classification of the present organizational status, and future considerations. To gain insight from all team members, both team and nonteam members, a SWOT analysis is recommended.

To do a SWOT analysis, Mike can follow these guidelines:

- *Guideline One:* Establish four (or more, depending on the number of people participating) teams whose work centers on each aspect of SWOT.
- *Guideline Two.* Regroup, with each team sharing its discoveries.
- *Guideline Three.* Break up into new groups prioritizing strengths, weaknesses, opportunities, and threats.

- *Guideline Four.* Regroup with all members, and use what you discovered about weaknesses to develop a focus.
- *Guideline Five.* Prioritize and agree upon what areas the team as a whole will work on bolstering.
- *Guideline Six.* Develop both short- and long-term plans.

REFLECTION

What does a SWOT analysis tell you about your school?

The audit we recommend is focused on outcomes. We believe that the only way a team can be measured is by assessing its performance in a quantitative construct. We mentioned many affiliative constructs in this chapter. They are important. However, they are important to the extent that they contribute to the quantitative growth of the organization. The team may feel good about themselves, but if they did not contribute to the overall effectiveness of the unit then the team is a failure. The following three-step procedure can be used to assess the team's effectiveness.

STEP 1: IDENTIFY THE TEAM'S MISSION, GOALS, AND OBJECTIVES

Each aspect of the mission, each goal and objective should be listed separately.

STEP 2: IDENTIFY THE SUCCESS CRITERIA FOR EACH ASPECT OF THE MISSION, GOAL, AND OBJECTIVE

The success criteria are those criteria that the group agrees meet the condition for successful completion of that component. A quantitative limit must be set. Mike may set 70% of an objective as indicating success. He may set the success rate higher or lower, depending on his environment.

STEP 3: EVALUATE THE IMPLEMENTATION OF
THE TEAM'S INITIATIVE

Identify each of the success criteria in the implementation. Identify each aspect where the success criterion was not met. Determine if the project was successful and make recommendations for further development.

The team process is simple. People work together for the good of their organization and for the good of each other. In its simplicity it is deceptively complex. At our best we work cooperatively. At our worst we can be selfish and ego centered. The supervisor's role is to move each member of the unit from selfishness to other centered. In the movement toward other centeredness the supervisor creates an environment where people learn that their survival is an interdependent consideration where reliance is based on trust, commitment, and relationships.

PULLING IT TOGETHER

FIELD BASED PROJECTS

1. Select three committees in your school setting. Collect meeting summaries, minutes, correspondence, and other artifacts that describe or report the workings of this team. Identify why this committee was formed. What types of work does this committee accomplish? What people comprise the committee? What authority does the committee have to make decisions? To whom does the committee report? What are the major accomplishments of this committee? What status is associated with being a member of this committee? How are the efforts and achievements of this committee rewarded by supervisors? Subordinates?

2. Reflect upon your experiences of being a member of a team. From your perspective, utilizing lessons learned from your experiences, can individuals accomplish more

than teams? Provide a specific context and give examples to support your response.

3. Develop policy and detailed procedures for rotating team membership for any major committee in your school setting. Be ready to present this policy and set of procedures to your supervisor for input and reaction. After presenting your ideas to your supervisor, modify the policy and procedures you developed to align more with the culture and context of your school. What potential derailers do you face implementing policy and procedure regarding team rotation?

FIELD BASED ANALYSIS

1. Interview an administrator who has recently assumed supervisory responsibility in a K–12 setting. Ask the following questions:
   - What types of teams were in place when he or she assumed the position?
   - What teams did this supervisor form? Why did the supervisor form these teams?
   - How did this supervisor decide who would serve on these teams?
   - How did the faculty respond to the way in which the supervisor made the decision on who would serve on these teams?
   - What obstacles did the supervisor face as he or she worked with teams?
   - How did this supervisor communicate teamwork to the rest of the faculty?
   - Did this supervisor ever deal with a dysfunctional team member? What course of action did the supervisor take in dealing with this team member? How did the rest of the team members respond to the supervisor's actions? Were there problems with this action? What were they?

2. Talk with two colleagues. Ask them to relate the rewards they gain from working in teams within their school set-

ting(s). How would they characterize the team's interactions with the supervisor or principal who is a member of the team? What makes this interaction positive? Negative?

3. If you do not belong to a school team or committee, ask your supervisor if you can attend a team/committee meeting. While at this meeting describe:

   ♦ The interactions between committee members. How do people interact with one another?

   ♦ How consensus is reached among members to any issues that are being discussed.

   ♦ If an administrator is a member of this committee/team, how do subordinates respond to him or her? Do subordinates respond differently to the supervisor than they do to fellow subordinates?

   ♦ From artifacts or statements, what type of preparation do you think the administrator did to prepare for the meeting?

   ♦ In your opinion, what was accomplished during this meeting?

   From this observation, what did you learn about the workings of teams regarding:

   ♦ Communication;

   ♦ Reaching consensus; and

   ♦ Making decisions.

IF YOU WERE MIKE SORELLI...

How would you encourage reluctant teachers to get involved in the work of teams?

How would you utilize the principal's advisory board to promote the development of teams at Milton Elementary?

What would you want to accomplish during the first meeting of this team?

How would you respond to a faction of teachers who believed you were wrong about joining the efforts of the team in developing both the school improvement plan and the 5-year plan?

How would you handle two team members who could not get along with one another?

How would you support the efforts of the team as they worked to develop the school improvement plan?

How would you get input from the faculty to present to this team?

What would you do to get the team ready to make decisions?

How would you work with the team to get them ready to present the draft copy of the school improvement plan?

How would you determine what values motivate you to action?

How would you assess the work of this team?

How would you protect the team's time?

How would you utilize the SWOT process?

How would you deal with a team member who was complacent? Overly critical? Dishonest during team meetings? Sabotaging the efforts of the team behind the scenes?

What would you consider before intervening?

RESOURCES FOR SUPERVISORS

BOOKS

Ackerman, R.H., Donaldson, G.A., Jr., & Van Der Bogert, R., *Making Sense as a School Leader: Persisting Questions, Creative Opportunities.* San Francisco: Jossey-Bass (1996).

Douglass, M.E. & Douglass, D.N., *Time Management for Teams.* New York: American Management Association (1992).

Larson, C.E. & LaFasto, F.M., *Teamwork: What Must Go Right/What Can Go Wrong.* CA: Sage Publications (1989).

WEB SITE

http://ericir.sunsite.syr.edu (Ask ERIC. Education information for research and development, data bases, and access to a virtual library).

7

SUCCESSFUL INSTRUCTIONAL SUPERVISION FOR SUPERVISORS

BUILDING BLOCKS

Effectiveness
Models
Culture
Ethics

INTRODUCTION

The classroom is the heart of the school. In the classroom, students and teacher come together for the purpose of learning. Within each classroom a series of interactions take place. When these interactions are planned, encourage inquiry, stimulate reflection, are driven by a high set of expectations, and girded by a teacher belief system based on the affirmation of the student's dignity, learning takes place. Supervision assists the teacher in facilitating this process. At its best, it contributes to teacher growth and sustains student growth. At its worst, it is punitive, misused, and misunderstood. Effective supervisors never use the supervisory process in a punitive manner. Effective supervisors fully understand the use of the supervisory process. Effective supervisors always affirm the nature of the learning experience and contribute to the continued personal and professional growth of the teacher and the emotional and intellectual growth of the student.

Supervision provides a baseline of data to assist teachers by providing learning opportunities and professional growth. The success of a supervisor is dependent, in part, on knowledge and professional qualities. These qualities encompass trust, loyalty, authenticity, and credibility. Effective supervisory practices are also dependent on the supervisor's knowledge about models of instructional supervision (e.g., clinical, coaching, peer review models) and their application. Knowledgeable supervisors distinguish between supervision and evaluation practices and processes when working with teachers. Finally, effective supervisors know the fundamentals of clear communications and building strong relationships with their faculty. As Good and Brophy state, "Principals can help classrooms function more productively by making teaching more satisfying and stimulating—a profession rather than an occupation that requires the performance of a limited number of classroom skills."[1]

This knowledge, coupled with professional qualities, assists the supervisor in assuming a collaborative responsibility with the teacher to enhance professional development. The indicators of "good" teaching are highlighted. "Good" teaching is not an accident. It is a strategically designed operation that is driven by effective teaching and complementary supervisory practices.

As you read this chapter, examine the various concepts presented. Reflect on the actions of the person in the supervision situation. Ask yourself if this person used the building blocks of effective instructional supervision, and how the building blocks mentioned in the chapter may have been more effectively utilized. Constantly ask yourself, "What should the supervisor do?" and, "How should the supervisor do it differently?"

SUPERVISION SITUATION

Angie Reynolds is the new principal at Mendelssohn Middle School. Mendelssohn Middle School enrolls 1,100 students, 96 full-time teachers, and 2 assistant principals. The previous principal, Martin Simmons, served Mendelssohn for 15 years and was appointed the Assistant Superintendent for Secondary Education. He is Angie's supervisor.

Although Angie is new to the district, she has 12 years of middle school teaching experience. The superintendent was impressed with Angie's background in middle school curriculum and instructional strategies. He assumed that because Angie was an excellent teacher, she would be able to work well with the staff at Mendelssohn. On hiring Angie, he stressed that he wanted an instructional leader who would be

---

[1] Thomas L. Good and Jere Brophy, *Looking in Classrooms* (7th ed.). New York: Longman (1997), p. 447.

actively involved with supervising teachers and promoting professional development. Angie accepted the challenge and began to develop a plan for working with her teachers. Her plan included restructuring the work of the assistant principals so that she could spend most of her time in the classroom observing instruction. Angie is convinced that she needs to do this to establish herself as an instructional leader. After reviewing district policy regarding supervisory and evaluation practices, Angie came to the conclusion that the records maintained by her predecessor provided little indication of teacher strengths and areas for continued development. Undaunted, she proceeded with her plan to develop a comprehensive program of teacher support and development. Her plan is simple. She has a vision of good teaching. Her supervisory efforts will conform to district guidelines and take into account the unique needs of her faculty and staff. Angie will share this plan at the first faculty meeting.

REFLECTION

How would you respond to your superintendent if given a similar charge?

RECOGNIZING "GOOD" TEACHING

TEACHING OCCURS IN A CLASSROOM CONTEXT

Angie Reynolds has made an assumption about her experience as a teacher and its relationship to her new role as a supervisor. She believes that because she was a good teacher, she can recognize good teaching in others. This is a common derailer for many supervisors. They project their idealized version of good teaching on others. In their projection, they assume that they are the ideal. And, if they are the ideal, then all other teachers should model their classroom behavior on their behavior. This false assumption contributes to the mistrust that exists between teachers and supervisors. Angie can correct this false assumption by recognizing that there are multiple teaching models that are effective. And that effectiveness is quantitatively measured through data that are collected during classroom observations and through assessment of the student performance using a documented standard for intellectual, social, and emotional growth. The practice of instructional supervision takes place in and outside of the classroom. Its goal is simple, yet its process is complex. Angie first needs to explore the classroom context.

CLASSROOM ENVIRONMENTS ARE COMPLEX

Angie needs to understand the specific and unique classroom context variables that affect teaching and learning. She needs to know her teachers, their instructional style, and teacher–learner relationships. All of these, when blended, form the classroom context. Within this context, each classroom has its own climate, culture, and human characteristics.

To understand the learning environment, Angie needs to examine how each variable (climate, culture, and characteristics) shapes instruction and learning. While observing in classrooms, Angie can look for climate indicators. Good and Brophy's process-outcome research suggests that Angie should focus on *teacher expectations, student opportunities to learn, classroom management and organization, curriculum pacing, active teaching, teaching to mastery, and evidence of a supportive learning environment.*[2]

REFLECTION

What are the characteristics that you associate with effective teaching? Why?

---

[2] *Ibid.,* pp. 361–362.

WHAT IS "EFFECTIVE" TEACHING?

A large body of research identifies effective teaching practices that promote learning. This body of research continues to grow as a result of continued and ongoing research on teaching and learning for both adults and school-aged children. Angie should rely on the major findings as guideposts. Barak Rosenshine's early research indicates that effective teaching can be identified by the behaviors of the teacher and the impact these behaviors have on learning. According to Rosenshine, effective teaching follows a set pattern that alternately includes a review, presentation, guided practice, correction and feedback, independent practice, and weekly and monthly reviews.[3]

TIP

Always adapt supervision models to fit your context.

Madeline Hunter extended Rosenshine's work and still exerts considerable influence on the instructional pattern (framework) that is still widely used today. Hunter's model closely follows Rosenshine's framework but extends the presentation aspect to include providing an anticipatory set and modeling.[4] Other instructional models and approaches, such as cooperative learning and mastery learning, have the capacity to increase student achievement. Charlotte Danielson developed an instructional framework encompassing four distinct domains of teaching responsibility and activity before,

---

[3] Barak V. Rosenshine, "Synthesis of Research on Explicit Teaching." *Educational Leadership*, 43, No. 7 (1986), p. 60.

[4] Madeline Hunter, *Mastery Teaching: Increasing Instructional Effectiveness in Elementary, Secondary Schools, Colleges and Universities.* El Segundo, CA: TIP Publications (1986).

during, and after teaching has occurred: "(1) planning and preparation; (2) classroom environment; (3) instruction; and (4) professional responsibility."[5] Danielson believes that a teaching framework, regardless of which is chosen, has the capacity to reap rewards, "A framework for professional practice can be used for a wide range of purposes, from meeting novices' needs to enhancing veterans' skills."[6]

The more Angie becomes familiar with research regarding effective teaching the more effective she becomes as an instructional supervisor. It is from this knowledge base that Angie can develop an accurate definition of good teaching. As the instructional leader, Angie needs to focus her energies on developing a definition of "good" teaching that is acceptable to her staff, students, and community. In the end, "good teaching" is effective teaching. Good teaching may or may not be matched to a person's likes or dislikes. It simply comes down to the teacher's impact on the children. The task of identifying effective teaching is time consuming. There are many aspects that need to be examined. These steps facilitate this process.

STEP 1: EXAMINE DOCUMENTS

Before taking any formal action, Angie needs to examine such artifacts as accreditation reports, curriculum guides, meeting summaries, past formative and summative observation reports from the prior principal, parent organization newsletters, awards and recognition of the faculty, staff, and students. These documents will give Angie insights into the academic program.

---

[5] Charlotte Danielson, *Enhancing Professional Practice: A Framework for Teaching*. Alexandria, VA: Association for Supervision and Curriculum Development (1996), p. 3.

[6] *Ibid.*, p. 2.

STEP 2: ENTER INTO DIALOGUE

Angie needs to consult with assistant principals, department chairs, teachers, students, parents—everyone associated with the instructional and academic program. She needs to create a history of past practices, emotions tied to the supervisory practice, and teacher understanding of the process.

STEP 3: EXTEND THE DIALOGUE

Instruction, learning, and classroom environments are complex; therefore, Angie needs to devote time during faculty meetings to engage the faculty in conversation about effective teaching. Out of these conversations staff development initiatives can be pursued. Angie needs to lead a facilitative process whereby teachers are engaged in conversations regarding effective teaching, more so than dictating the precepts of effective teaching.

REFLECTION

How much time has been spent in your school discussing effective instruction? How do you account for this?

STEP 4: DEVOTE TIME FOR TEACHERS TO DEVELOP AND DEFINE EFFECTIVE TEACHER TRAITS

Angie can capitalize on the experiences and strengths of her faculty by encouraging small-group work discussions by grade level and subject area regarding effective teaching practices. The work of small groups can be shared in large groups so the entire school can begin to extend the conversation and to share what they have learned.

STEP 5: OBSERVE TEACHERS IN THEIR ENVIRONMENT

Angie needs to base the new program on the needs of the members of Mendelssohn Middle School. She can do this by being cooperatively involved with teachers in the instructional process. Angie needs to observe teachers regularly, both formally and informally. Early visitations can give a sense of strengths and of areas in need of bolstering. Ineffective supervisors do not consider classroom supervision as an integral part of their strategic plan. Angie should expect some anxiety about the principal entering the classroom. Continued and ongoing visibility helps reduce anxiety encountered when a new principal assumes the role of instructional supervisor.

STEP 6: DEVELOP A SCHOOLWIDE PROFILE WHICH INCLUDES EFFECTIVE TEACHER CHARACTERISTICS

Effective teachers know their subject matter, are prepared mentally and physically to teach, understand their learning environment, and promote student learning through active participation in a variety of activities. By utilizing multiple teaching strategies, they connect course and content matter with everyday applications, care about children, and are risk-takers in trying new learning strategies.[7] This profile becomes the standard against which Angie and her teachers measure the teaching effectiveness which occurs in the Mendelson classrooms.

STEP 7: DESCRIBE TEACHING PRACTICES THAT COMPLEMENT EFFECTIVE TEACHER CHARACTERISTICS

The cooperative learning model is an example of teaching practice that is grounded in the effective teaching characteristic and promotes student learning through active participation in a variety of activities by using multiple teaching strategies. For example, Mendelssohn Middle School teachers describe the impact of the cooperative learning model as one where stu-

---

[7] In *Techniques in the Clinical Supervision of Teachers: Pre-Service and In-Service Applications* ((4th ed.) New York: Longman (1997)), Kieth A. Acheson and Meredith Damien Gall provide a list of effective teaching characteristics, which includes many of the items we suggest.

dents take responsibility for their learning and apply previously learned knowledge to a variety of contexts, and where teachers use multiple learning strategies to impact student learning. Angie must realize that any model is only as effective as the teacher who implements the model. An effective model poorly implemented will not produce positive results. Angie's teachers must believe in the efficacy of the model and have a personal belief in their capabilities to implement the model effectively.

STEP 8: CONNECT OBSERVATIONS AND GROUP DISCUSSIONS WITH OTHER RELATED ACTIVITIES

As the instructional leader, Angie controls the agenda in terms of the conversation. Her continued focus on instruction links what happens in the classroom to faculty meetings, staff development, and parent conferences. It is an integrated process. When this process is fully integrated teachers feel more professional and become diagnosticians of a craft. They no longer see themselves as technicians with limited abilities.

STEP 9: ALIGN SUPERVISORY PRACTICES WITH TEACHER RESPONSIBILITY

Angie should focus on the teachers' professional development growth by continuously focusing on teacher responsibility. Angie is not responsible for effective teaching. However, many people inaccurately want to make Angie and other supervisors responsible for this task. Responsibility for effective teaching rests with each teacher. Angie's primary responsibility is to facilitate this process. When Angie assumes this responsibility, she denigrates the dignity associated with teaching. When Angie affirms the teacher's responsibility to seek to become more effective, she attests to the dignity of the teacher.

REFLECTION

To what extent do you believe that teachers are encouraged to be responsible for effective teaching? How do you account for this?

SELECTING A SUPERVISORY MODEL THAT FITS THE CONTEXTUAL AND ORGANIZATIONAL NEEDS OF YOUR SCHOOL

KNOW YOUR PEOPLE AND THEIR NEEDS

Angie is committed to crafting a building-level supervisory plan that complies with district guidelines. Her plan is one that takes into account the unique needs of her faculty and staff. On one hand, Angie is to be commended for her advance planning. On the other hand, Angie may be creating unnecessary problems. Consider her situation. Angie is operating from a vertical perspective, one that is driven by a top-down perspective. This top-down perspective has generated a narrow perspective of the supervisory needs at her school. When Angie holds to her narrow perspective, she runs the risk of forming inaccurate assumptions. One assumption that Angie made was that she should reconfigure the roles of the assistant principals so that she would be solely responsible for supervising teachers. Angie believes that she has developed a supervisory plan that her teachers will accept. Her assumption has left her vulnerable to criticism.

Angie must widen her focus and shift from a top-down perspective to one that includes both top-down and horizontal input. Angie operates horizontally by asking critical questions of her faculty that help determine instructional needs. Together, they examine how to build an environment where student learning and teacher growth compliment each other.

TIP

Never underestimate your faculty's instructional ability.

To accomplish these objectives, Angie and her faculty should focus their attention on the following five items:

THE EXPERIENCE LEVEL OF THE FACULTY AND STAFF

Angie needs to know the experience levels of her faculty, the prior experiences of her staff, the length of service her teachers have given to Mendelssohn Middle School, and the effectiveness of the previous staff development activities. Angie realizes that the number of classroom observations has little, if any, relationship to good teaching. She knows that classroom observations must be coupled with useful information presented in ways in which the teacher will readily assimilate and apply the information.[8]

PREVIOUS SCHOOLWIDE INITIATIVES

To assess the needs of her faculty and staff, Angie needs to understand schoolwide initiatives. For example, if Mendelssohn Middle School is in the process of implementing the instructional model of cooperative learning to reach reluctant learners, Angie needs to know where the faculty is in relationship to implementing cooperative learning, how long the initiative has been in place, what types of training and staff development the faculty had in cooperative learning, and what role her predecessor had in facilitating the process. Angie and her faculty will need to determine the types of additional faculty support to implement the program.

---

[8] Good and Brophy, *op. cit.*

PAST SUPERVISORY PRACTICES

For Angie to understand her teachers and their attitudes and beliefs about supervision, she needs to know and understand the experiences they had with previous supervisory processes. Her teachers' views of supervision will be based on their experience. Many will assume that Angie will implement the traditional supervisory model. The traditional supervisory model that most teachers' experience is obligatory in nature and seldom tied to good practice. It is obligatory in that the supervisor (in most cases the building principal) is required to make specified observations and evaluations. Once obligatory requirements are met, instructional supervision is no longer important. This is not the fault of principals. Angie will learn that her day is filled with interactions. The typical principal has over 400 separate interactions each day. It is difficult for a principal to give consistent primacy to instructional supervision as a core activity. This is precisely the reason we seek to place the responsibility for effective teaching on the teacher and define the supervisor's role as one of facilitating this process.

THE ORGANIZATION'S EXISTING SUPERVISORY PROGRAM

Angie needs to know the organizational structure of the building and district in which she works. Moreover, she needs to know the types of supervisory and evaluative practices that have been followed, why these practices have been followed, and the results of these practices. Angie needs to understand the district's expectations. There are three steps that Angie can follow to clarify district policies.

STEP 1: EXAMINE DISTRICT POLICY

When Angie examines district policy, she should look for information on the frequency and length of observation, formal and informal observations, union agreements, time frames for completion of the evaluation process, and delineated district standards for effective teaching.

STEP 2: SEEK INSIGHTS FROM OTHER PRINCIPALS AND DISTRICT-LEVEL ADMINISTRATORS

Angie needs to discover how teachers in the district respond to the culturally driven supervision process. The process is culturally driven if the faculty and administration have unwritten assumptions as to how supervision is conducted. She can discover these assumptions by asking questions related to the number and type of grievances that were filed related to supervisory practices (in her building and in other buildings) within her district. She can inquire as to the support that instructional supervisors received from superordinates in the past. She can inquire about the primacy that the district places on instructional supervision. Is the district's concern motivated by a political agenda, or is it driven by a desire to promote teacher effectiveness and student learning?

REFLECTION

How do your district's policies contribute to or detract from effective instruction?

STEP 3: CONSULT WITH OTHER BUILDING-LEVEL SUPERVISORS

Since Angie has assistant principals, she needs to consult with them to discover their roles in the supervisory process. Angie unilaterally decided that she would assume sole responsibility for supervising instructional practices. She might reconsider this policy and place instructional supervision into a broader context. If Angie chooses to accept the role of facilitator of effective instruction, her colleagues need to be brought into this model. They need to be apprenticed to a paradigm that breaks with past practices that focused on the supervisor as responsible and the teacher as accountable, with little of either occurring.

EXAMINE SUPERVISORY MODELS AND THEIR COMPONENTS

Angie needs to determine if the supervisory model(s) used by the district are linked to best practice regarding the professional growth of teachers. District policies generally define instructional supervision in terms of teacher evaluation. Evaluation processes are identified as formative and summative in nature. "Formative" means "ongoing" or in "progress." During the formative stages of supervision, Angie and the teacher work collaboratively to enhance the teacher's professional growth. Summative is the final outcome. Angie uses her formative assessments to connect to her summative evaluation. In schools, a series of summative judgments are based upon the meanings derived from the formative or ongoing efforts unfolding over time in the teacher's classroom. Supervisory models are formative in nature. Summative procedures are generally related to policy and the need of the district to make employment determinations.

Consider the following supervisory models that have evolved over time: clinical supervision (Goldhammer, 1969; Cogan, 1973); peer coaching (Joyce & Showers, 1982); peer supervision (Alphonso & Goldsberry, 1982); and cognitive coaching (Costa, 1994). With varying degree and emphasis, these models have common attributes such as the preobservation conference, the observation, and the postobservation conference as part of the model, regardless of whether the supervisor or a peer is utilizing the model.

Many districts use a menu approach to develop their districtwide or building-level supervisory practices, picking and choosing attributes from several different models to create their own model of supervision. This picking and choosing assists with developing context-specific supervisory practices. The end results are the development of strategies that are situation based. This is why Angie needs to consider who her teachers are and where they are in their professional development.

CLINICAL SUPERVISION

A frequently used supervisory model is clinical supervision. The clinical supervision model developed by Goldhammer and Cogan is a process that includes three distinct phases—the preobservation conference, the classroom observation, and the postobservation conference.

PHASE ONE: THE PREOBSERVATION CONFERENCE

The preobservation conference is a critical aspect of any formal observation. It is during this conference that the *parameters* of what is to be observed are discussed. Angie and the teacher discuss the content that will be taught, the observation period, the context, the duration, and specific items that they bring to this conversation.

REFLECTION

What has been your experience with clinical supervision? Do you think that those who used this model were competent in its application? What makes you account for this opinion?

Once these technical aspects are determined, the supervisor and teacher can have a conversation about teaching and learning within the specific context of the classroom which includes the learners, their specific needs, and ability levels. By talking about the learners and their unique characteristics, Angie begins to understand the learning context. She needs to understand the type of instructional practices that will be used to meet instructional goals, the assessment techniques that measure student learning, and the classroom management strategies to achieve the lesson's objectives. This conversation includes the areas that the teacher would like Angie to focus on during the lesson. This focus enables the teacher and Angie to limit their focus. This is a collaborative process that is entered into by both parties to foster a conversation regarding the content and context of the observed instructional period.

PHASE TWO: THE OBSERVATION

The classroom observation is the time when Angie, with undivided attention, expends energy collecting data. She needs to determine how to collect data that will be useful to the teacher. There are some guidelines that Angie can follow.

♦ Angie can use seating charts to chronicle teacher questions, student responses, and classroom traffic.

♦ Angie can use a watch to track activities and time (question-and-answer sequence, cooperative learning work in small and large groups, lecture, guided practice, and independent practice).

♦ Angie can develop charts that assist tracking information.

PHASE THREE: THE POSTOBSERVATION CONFERENCE

We believe the most important phase of the clinical supervisory model is the postobservation conference. The postobservation conference is where the data collected during the observation are presented in such a way that the teacher can understand what was observed, process the data, reflect upon the data in relation to current practices, and brainstorm refinement of classroom practices.

The postobservation conference can be characterized as a period of analysis. Analysis should occur with the teacher taking the lead in analyzing and reflecting upon practice. Effective supervisors resist the temptation to analyze observation data by attaching value judgments about what was observed prior to conducting the postobservation conference. More self-perspective is gained if the teacher is afforded the opportunity to think and reflect upon their teaching practice. During the postobservation conference, the focus becomes a means to generate dialogue. The postobservation conference is really a conversation about teaching and learning. This conversation focuses on what happened during the classroom observation. Angie and the teacher have to reach agreement on the reality of the observation. Angie cannot impose her reality on the teacher any more than she can accept the teacher's reference point. The conversation is a way to reach common ground as to what occurred. Once Angie and the teacher reach agreement on what happened, they discuss, reflectively, the instructional process. In this sense, Angie acts as the facilitator, drawing out of the teacher the rationale behind the teacher's actions, alternatives the teacher might consider if they were replaying the same incident, and an awareness of how teacher actions influenced the dynamics of the class. Angie is at her best when the teacher volunteers this information. She is at her worst when she dictates what happened, what should have happened, and what the teacher is expected to do in the future.

REFLECTION

What have your experiences been with your post-observation conferences? How did you leave these conferences? Were you invigorated? Did you feel like you learned something? Or were you just happy the process was finished? How do you account for your answers?

According to Zepeda, effective supervisors "get supervision out of the main office"[9] by conducting postobservation conferences in teachers' classrooms where observations occurred. Conducting the postobservation conference in the teacher's classroom enables the teacher to better visualize the events chronicled in the supervisor's notes.

---

[9] Sally J. Zepeda, "How to Ensure Positive Responses in Classroom Observations: Tips for Principals." *NASSP*, May 1995, pp. 1–2.

Time is critical. Effective supervisors conduct timely postobservation conferences. For example, Bellon and Bellon urge supervisors and teachers to reconstruct the events of the observation on the same day as the classroom observation. This technique, referred to as "lesson reconstruction," is one way to assist teacher thinking with a fresh memory about the events of the classroom.

PEER-MEDIATED SUPERVISORY MODELS

Since the early 1980s, several promising models of peer-oriented supervision have emerged. Peer-mediated models of supervision have gained ground with the renewed view of teachers as capable professionals who have a great deal to offer one another. Research has yielded positive support regarding the impact of teachers assisting teachers to improve classroom performance. The processes of peer supervision (Alphonso and Goldsberry, 1982), coaching (Joyce and Showers, 1982), and other forms, such as cognitive coaching (Costa, 1994), involve the underpinnings of clinical supervision, and have been shown to increase levels of interaction and communication between teachers.

Supervision in itself is not a discrete activity. As McQuarrie and Wood indicated, "Supervision, staff development, and teacher evaluation are more than three distinct, independent processes that can be employed to improve instruction. They should all be considered part of a comprehensive approach to improve instructional practices."[10] Peer-mediated models of supervision have the capacity to include the teacher in all aspects of their professional growth as an active participant instead of an observer on the sidelines. They also contribute to teacher responsibility for self and profession.

---

[10] Frank O. McQuarrie, Jr., and Fred H. Wood, "Supervision, Staff Development, and Evaluation Connections." *Theory into Practice*, vol. XXX, No. 2 (1991), p. 94.

Although peer-mediated supervisory models are designed to promote collaboration, feedback, guidance, and perspective, these models do not preclude Angie from participating with her teachers in this model. Angie may want to explore collegial forms of assistance by examining the culture, climate, and context of her organization to determine the efficacy of such efforts. According to McQuarrie and Wood, readying the people and the organization simultaneously is critical if change is going to have any lasting impact.[11] If Angie becomes committed to supporting this type of change, she needs to empower her teachers. She would, as a beginning point, need to determine if her faculty and staff were willing to undertake this professional responsibility. If her faculty and staff committed to these types of practices, then they would need opportunities for initial training, ongoing support at the building level, support from central administration (e.g., superintendent and curriculum coordinators), the union, and other special interest groups.

REFLECTION

What are the strengths and weaknesses of the peer-mediated model? Would you trust your peers to evaluate you? Why?

DEVELOPING NEW SUPERVISORY PRACTICES

If her teachers are willing to extend their involvement to alternative forms of supervision (e.g., coaching, portfolio, mentoring), Angie needs to initiate the process of charting changes in supervisory practices by gathering information to make decisions about current supervisory practices. She can do this by following this six-step process.

---

[11] *Ibid.*

> **TIP**
>
> Move slowly while educating, informing, and coaching with each step.

STEP 1: BEGIN SLOWLY

Angie needs to gather information. This information can be gathered through a variety of means. The most effective means is through a series of focus groups. A needs assessment is a less effective means. Angie needs to determine the level of understanding of the supervisory process, the willingness to accept responsibility for effective teaching, and the commitment to professional development. If Angie discovers that the faculty is operating under misconceived notions regarding supervision, she will have to construct an education process that gradually alters the attitudes of the teachers toward supervision. Without proper faculty understanding of the process, Angie will fail in her attempts to construct an effective supervision process. If Angie discovers that the faculty believes supervision is the supervisor's job, then Angie will again have to work with the faculty to gradually transform their attitude toward personal responsibility for effective teaching. As faculty acceptance of responsibility increases, Angie's role gradually is transformed to that of facilitator. And if Angie discovers that the faculty is not concerned with professional development, she will have to discover the source of this attitude. Perhaps staff development in the past was poorly conceived, lacking follow-through, and providing insufficient coaching. Angie can do something about each of these issues. However, in every case, she has to begin slowly and move toward her optimum goal.

STEP 2: ANALYZING DATA WITH FACULTY AND STAFF

The more faculty are involved in studying current practice and its impact on their professional development, the more likely they are to take the lead in making modifications. This will increase ownership and reduce anxiety in the change.

Study teams can be formed in departments, at grade levels, voluntarily, and in cross-discipline or cross-grade levels.

STEP 3: DETERMINE A LOGICAL STARTING POINT

Angie may decide to initiate the supervision process with newly hired teachers or those with less than 5 years experience. The starting point is arbitrary. However, we believe that there should be two points of initiation. The first point is aligned with school district policy. Some districts have specific guidelines as to who will be evaluated and who will not be evaluated. Angie must adhere to this policy. If there are no such guidelines, Angie must initially focus on teachers who have been identified as marginal players. She has a responsibility to the students and parents to insure effective instruction. Angie acts ethically when she moves to eliminate marginal and substandard teaching practices.

STEP 4: KEEP ALL PARTIES INFORMED OF EFFORTS AND CHANGES

Angie needs to allow a faculty review of any changes in supervisory practices. This documentation should be sent to district level administrators for feedback and in conformity with school district policy. Depending on district policy, formal approval by the board of education to institute changes in supervisory practices might be needed. Often, supervisory procedures are tied to policies, state regulations, the union, and contract agreements.

STEP 5: MONITOR THE PLAN'S PROGRESS

Monitoring strategies needs to be balanced between informal and formal measures. Formal measures include examining documents, artifacts, and changes in practice. For example, a principal instituted a peer review program for tenured teachers interested in self-supervision. Teachers who paired up to do peer reviews were required to fill out a simple form each time they observed one another. Completed forms were kept on file in the principal's office. Oftentimes supervisors initiate practices that sound exciting on paper and realize to their chagrin that the practice is more complex than they had thought. Peer review is one such process. Before beginning this practice or any other practice make sure that those participating in the process are adequately trained. The best way to ruin a good idea is to move forward without adequate training.

STEP 6: EVALUATION

Angie will need to set standards regarding any new supervisory process. The basic standard that must be used is: Are the students learning more since the program has been in place than they were previous to its inception? If the students are not learning more, the program is not effective. This "bottom line" approach speaks to the currency of education. It is a currency of human capital that cannot be replaced by affiliative goals. As much as it is important for teachers to be positive about the process, it is much more important for students to learn. Any supervisory system that does not demonstratively contribute to student learning is not effective.

GUIDELINES FOR SUPERVISORS

Supervision should be a positive process for those being supervised. Angie needs to be a leader who supports teachers and their efforts in the classroom. Ideally, she needs to have a plan of action to encourage the faculty to play a major role in planning their professional development. More importantly, Angie needs to understand how her role can change as she works with teachers. Consider Angie's position. She does not know her faculty and staff, nor does she have a history with the school or the district. Her words, actions, and deeds communicate her role to her staff. Angie's actions need to be value driven. If her values are other-centered, we believe that she will succeed. If her values are self-centered, she will have a difficult time convincing the faculty of her sincerity.

Angie needs to demonstrate competence in the application of supervisory skills. If Angie is incompetent, the faculty will not trust her assessment or recommendations. Competence is the foundation of professional respect. If Angie lacks the essential competencies, she must find the resources to acquire these skills. Then Angie must remember, *competence is gained through practice, practice, practice.*

There are specific characteristics needed to fulfill the role of instructional supervisor. Angie must be *flexible.* Schools and their people are constantly changing. To manage change and its implications for teachers, she needs to be flexible. Ineffective supervisors are rigid, inconsistent, poor decision-makers, and lack integrity. When Angie is flexible, she understands boundaries, roles, and policies. She is able to probe, stretch, and challenge within these parameters. The rubber band is stretched but never broken.

Angie needs to be intuitive. When Angie is intuitive, she know her faculty. She intuitively knows how to lead her teachers in meeting instructional needs and concerns. When we speak of intuition, we speak of the ability to listen with her head and interpret the message through her heart. This "heart-filtered" intuitive approach will result in better instructional practices that support and/or enhance student learning and achievement.

Angie needs to be knowledgeable. When Angie is knowledgeable, she has a complex and expanding knowledge base. Her knowledge comes from many sources such as discussions with teachers and other district processionals, reading professional journals, attending conferences, updating knowledge through graduate classes, and accessing information electronically. Angie needs to continually update her skills and engage in activities that enhance her professional development and knowledge.

Angie must be willing to accept divergent views and methods. When Angie is open to divergent views and methods regarding instruction, she is able to explore a wide variety of paradigms. No two teachers teach the same lesson the same way. Angie's openness empowers teachers to experiment with instruction and assessment, classroom management strategies, and the curriculum.

REFLECTION

What is the most outstanding characteristic that your current supervisor exhibits in the instructional supervision process? What characteristic is lacking in the instructional supervision process?

DETERMINING YOUR SUPERVISORY ROLE

Angie needs to identify her values and beliefs about teaching, teachers, and learners (both students and adults). Angie has the responsibility for supervising the people in her building. If Angie has not identified her core values, she will not be able to consistently send a positive message in her supervisory dealings with subordinates. Angie needs to determine if she will act as a critic. If she acts as a critic, she remains detached and assesses a "performance" without allowing personal bias to cloud the flow of data. The critic's role is to accurately name reality.

If Angie acts as a coach, she will be a quiet observer picking out strengths and weaknesses with a finely tuned eye. She will not miss opportunities for positive reinforcement or to correct misapplied techniques or strategies. When Angie acts as a coach, she serves as a dynamic leader in a vibrant organization. According to Jack Callahan, a career veteran of Sears' Allstate Insurance Company, "Good coaches help us explore our capacity to grow."[12] Sometimes coaches have to make tough calls; sometimes they lead team members through practice, praise, and encouragement to perfect skills; and some-

---

[12] John D. Callahan, in Robert H. Rosen with Paul B. Brown, *Leading People: Transforming Business from the Inside Out.* New York: Viking Penguin (1996), p. 359.

times coaches have to do more than gently nudge their players into realizing their potential. When Angie acts as a coach she also becomes a champion of effective teaching.

SUPERVISOR AS CHANGE AGENT

Angie acts as a change agent when she assists teachers in recognizing a need for change. Change occurs more effectively when Angie creates a safe environment, one where teachers are 1`willing to risk new techniques and strategies. From a supervisory perspective, the best type of change is member driven and occurs in small steps. Forced change has little long-term impact. Angie builds trusting relationships that create a climate and culture open to experimentation and risk taking when she approaches change constructively.

POLITICS AND INSTRUCTIONAL SUPERVISION

When supervising instruction, it is critical for Angie to distinguish between the understanding of politics and its application versus being secretive and manipulatory. When Angie understands the difference and prevents a political agenda from interfering with supervisory practices, she builds a climate of trust. Angie's present situation is one that is fraught with political intrigue. Her superintendent wants supervision to be Angie's primary focus. Angie knows her performance will be judged on her ability to work well with teachers as they work on improving instruction. Yet, her immediate supervisor is the former principal of her school. He may have a political agenda that will not allow Angie to be successful. Similarly, the superintendent's focus on instructional supervision may be driven by a political agenda associated with school board politics. We believe that politics, as practiced in most communities, has no place in the instructional supervision process. Angie serves her faculty and school best by sidestepping these issues, acting with integrity, and adamantly refusing to allow political subterfuge to interfere with the supervisory process.

EVALUATING SUPERVISORY PRACTICES

Angie has to assess the effectiveness of her instructional supervision efforts. She needs to ask tough questions of herself as she examines the impact of her role as supervisor and of the processes and procedures inherent in the supervisory model used in her building. The questions that Angie asks need to be answered with data. The aim of such an inquiry should be to assess the effect of Angie's supervisory practices on instruction. Instruction can only be assessed by determining its impact on students. Angie needs to gather data that will lead her to descriptive information. We suggest Angie consider this four-step model.

REFLECTION

How would teachers in your school evaluate your current supervisor's instructional supervision capabilities? What advice would you give to your supervisor to be more effective?

STEP 1: LOOK FOR INDICATORS

Angie needs to record objective data such as the number of formal observations made, frequency of observations (look for trends such as number of visitations at the beginning, middle, or end of the year); number of informal observations made; teacher ratings (e.g., satisfactory, unsatisfactory, excellent; by subject and grade level; experience level); types of concrete recommendations made by the supervisor and those generated by teachers in postobservation conferences. In addition, she must consider the academic achievement of the students in each teacher's classroom as the primary source of information on teacher effectiveness. Without these data, other measures lack quality and depth.

STEP 2: EXAMINE SUPERVISORY FOLLOW-UP ACTIVITIES

Angie needs to examine the types of follow-up activities that she used to implement her coaching strategies. Coaching effectively takes time and presence. If Angie is an effective coach, she will see the change in behavior during the practice sessions. How well Angie conducts her practice sessions will impact the quality of instruction in the classroom. One way of measuring her effectiveness in these sessions is to videotape the sessions and review them with the teacher.

STEP 3: ASSESS TEACHER, STUDENT, AND PARENT OPINIONS REGARDING THE SCHOOL'S INSTRUCTIONAL PROGRAM

A student may not be able to describe why a teacher is good or marginal, but the student will be able to tell you if they are enjoying their learning experience. This kind of qualitative data is critical to Angie. Teachers, students, and parents will provide Angie with differing perspectives. Angie must integrate these differing viewpoints to gain an accurate picture.

STEP 4: LOOK FOR COMMON THEMES AND PATTERNS IN RESPONSES

Angie needs to include others in helping her make sense out of the data she has collected. In all cases, the data supply answers, problems, and a source of reality if used accurately. If Angie chooses to use the data to bolster her efforts by manipulating data, she wastes her time. Data should instruct. The more data instruct Angie, the more she can use the data to educate teachers to move toward more effective teaching strategies. Data allow Angie to move away from personality conflicts toward constructive collaboration.

ETHICAL ISSUES RELATING TO SUPERVISION

Supervision should be an objective process used to foster growth, professionalism, and competence. As a new supervisor, Angie faces many situations that will test her ethical and moral fiber. To act unethically or immorally as a supervisor will jeopardize her credibility with teachers, staff, parents, and student—the community. Calabrese and Calabrese-Barton state that the ethical standard that should be used is "....based on the metaphors of co-collaboration, journey, and process. [Where] the definition of ethics is a struggle that is joined in collaboratively where there is no final answer but a process toward a destination. It is more in the awareness of what we are doing and the effects that our actions have than in being assured that we have the right set of answers. It is a white water experience where certainty is nowhere to be found."[13]

Ethical actions are defined by the their outcomes. Angie and her faculty have to speak to the outcomes of their activity with a single voice. It is a voice that is not defensive, but a voice that seeks to honor the responsibility the community has given to them. It is a voice that seeks to live out its duty to construct an effective teaching and learning environment. It is a voice that seeks to rid the school of anything that detracts from honoring this responsibility and duty.

REFLECTION

How ethical is your supervisor in the instructional supervision process? Does your supervisor meet the standards set in this chapter?

---

[13] Raymond L. Calabrese and Angela Calabrese-Barton, "Reconceptualizing Ethics in Educational Administration Programs." In: J. Burdin, ed., *Leadership and Diversity in Education: The Second Yearbook of the National Council of Professors of Educational Administration*. Lancaster, PA: Technomic Publishing (1994), p. 132.

Instructional supervision is a critical component for the school supervisor. Supervisors like Angie need to understand that instructional supervision takes place in the greater context of leadership and management of their unit. Instructional supervision is not the context; it serves the context. It can only serve the context when Angie constructs a paradigm centered in teacher responsibility for effective teaching. In our experience, teachers accept responsibility when they are trusted to be responsible. They accept responsibility when they recognize that failure is an opportunity for coaching rather than criticizing. They accept responsibility when the supervisor sees them as competent and worthy of being a teacher.

PULLING IT TOGETHER

FIELD BASED PROJECTS

1. Seek permission from your building principal to shadow a preobservation conference, classroom observation, and postobservation conference with one or two colleagues who are willing to let you be a participant. Take notes on both the process and the content of the clinical supervisory process. Meet with the principal to gain his or her insights into the process you observed. Did you observe the same events as the supervisor? Does your assessment of the process match your principal's assessment?

2. Ask a colleague to videotape you teaching in your classroom. Watch this tape and then reflect on:
   ♦ What type of feedback would you want to hear about your lesson?
   ♦ How would you want this feedback presented?

   Do you see a value in using technology in assisting teachers grow professionally? What are the strengths and weaknesses of using technology as a supervisory tool?

3. Reflect on two supervisors who have supervised your classroom performance. Identify what patterns of behavior they exhibited that made them either effective or ineffec-

tive. What behaviors would you want to emulate? Avoid? Modify?

FIELD BASED ANALYSIS

1. Choose a school to analyze. Collect data on district policy relating to teacher supervision and evaluation. Collect instruments and forms used by supervisors to record formal and informal observation data at both the formative and summative levels. Analyze these documents. Identify the procedures and processes found within the policy statements that promote growth. Identify the procedures and processes found within the policy statements that deal with evaluation. Do any of the intents of these statements overlap with one another? Can the processes of supervision and evaluation complement one another given the organizational structure of this district?

2. Choose two work units within your school that have official supervisors. Ask the supervisors how their supervisory practices complement the overall supervision provided by the school principal (or whoever their designated superordinate is for that particular unit). Ask the supervisors what they do to eliminate sending conflicting messages to subordinates if there is disagreement about a subordinate's performance. From what you have learned, what is needed to avoid sending conflicting messages to subordinates from unit and larger school supervisors?

3. Select two supervisors from your school community. Ask each what they believe are the most important items to communicate regarding instructional supervision to their staff at the beginning of the year. What supervisory actions or deeds support their words? What supervisory actions or deeds detract from the message of their words? Then, ask two colleagues what they wish supervisors would tell them about classroom supervision. What are the similarities and differences? As a future supervisor, what would

you want to tell your faculty about supervision? What actions or deeds would help you support your words?

IF YOU WERE ANGIE REYNOLDS...

What clarifying questions would you want to ask your superintendent?

Why would it be advantageous for you to speak with Martin Simmons, the former principal of Mendelssohn Middle School?

How would you deal with the possible conflict with Martin Simmons?

How would you better utilize the talents of the assistant principals?

How would you communicate your vision about "good" teaching to your faculty?

What steps would you take to include the faculty in developing the picture of what "good" teaching is at Mendelssohn Middle School?

How would you discover what the professional needs are of your faculty?

What are some ways you would address individual needs through supervision?

Why would it be important to know how subordinates perceive supervision at Mendelssohn Middle School?

What steps would you take if a group of teachers approached you about the inadequacies of existing supervisory practices?

Whom would you include in the discussions about the possibility of changing supervisory practices at Mendelssohn Middle School?

Would you want to be known as a supervisor who is a coach? Critic? Change agent? Explain your choice.

What would you do if a superordinate asked you to keep an extra special eye on a veteran teacher who was generally at odds with the Mendelssohn Middle School community?

What would you do if a subordinate was making false accusations about your abilities to effectively supervise instruction?

RESOURCES FOR SUPERVISORS

BOOKS

Good, T.L. & Brophy, J.E., *Looking in Classrooms* (7th ed.). New York: Longman (1997).

Jennings, D.F., *Effective Supervision: Frontline Management for the 90s*. St. Paul, MN: West Publishing (1993).

Ornstein, A.C., *Teaching: Theory into Practice*. Boston, MA: Allyn & Bacon (1995).

Ornstein, A.C., *Strategies for Effective Teaching*. New York: HarperCollins (1990).

WEB SITE

http://www.ed.asu.edu/aera (Home page for the American Educational Research Association).

8

SUCCESSFUL COMMUNICATION AND POLITICAL SKILLS FOR SUPERVISORS

BUILDING BLOCKS

Communication
Politics
Fairness
Benchmarks

INTRODUCTION

One experience novice supervisors have in common is derailment. These supervisors have a broad knowledge base and want desperately to succeed; however, they still fail. If you had the chance to talk to them about their unpleasant experiences, and were able to probe into the events that surrounded their derailment, you would discover that they lacked skills in two areas: *communication* and *politics*. Both skills are critical if the supervisor is to work effectively with *difficult people* and in *difficult situations*. College courses provide the supervisor with knowledge. Knowledge is the water stored in a large lake behind a dam before it is processed through the hydroelectric plant. If the water is not allowed to flow through a hydroelectric plant, it has great potential, but produces no electrical benefit. This chapter is designed to help you take your knowledge of communication and politics and transform it into an energy force. On one hand, we are giving you knowledge. On the other hand, it is a practical knowledge. It is an applied knowledge. You will find situations that you will likely encounter as a supervisor. The communication and political skills that we share with you will guide you in this process. When we speak of political skills, we are not speaking in the context of elections or political skills as we see them being applied through the media. In most cases, what is observed in the media is the blatant abuse of power and manipulative attempts to coerce or force people to accept a message (communication) that is unacceptable. This is the *dark side* of politics. We prefer to view politics from a positive perspective. It is a process where the supervisor uses politics as an art form where people with divergent, often discordant, views are brought together to work for a shared purpose. This brings us to the complementary skill of communication. Communication transcends the technical skills of writing, speaking, and active listening. Obviously, you cannot communicate without technical skills. However, communication includes ideas, image, attitude, presence, projection, and identification. You can speak well, but if you are not communicating your ideas and stimulating the political process, you are not effectively communicating or politically effective. We like a white-water canoeing metaphor. For example, imagine that you and a friend are in a two-person canoe and enter into a stretch of white-water. The person sitting in the rear of the canoe has the responsibility to steer the canoe (political skills) through the rapids. The person in the front of the canoe paddles, giving thrust and calling out the danger of rocks to the person steering the canoe (communication skills). If either person fails to hold to his or her responsibility, the canoe will overturn, endangering both members. If you learn to use these skills you will decrease your chances of derailment and improve the effectiveness of your unit. As you read this chapter, examine the various concepts that are presented. Reflect on the actions of the person in the supervision situation. Ask yourself if this person is using the building blocks to effective supervision and how the building blocks mentioned in this chapter may be more effectively placed. Constantly ask yourself, "What should the supervisor do?" and, "How should the supervisor do it differently?"

SUPERVISION SITUATION

Carmela McKenzie is having a white-water experience. A week ago, Carmela was an assistant principal in an elementary school. She worked for a principal she admired. The principal served as her mentor, provided her with increasing levels of responsibilities, and made her feel a partner in the school's administration. It was an idyllic setting. Student achievement scores were high, teachers were happy, and the parents were actively involved. Carmela was content to spend her career in this situation. That all changed when the superintendent spoke personally to Carmela and asked her to take over the principalship at Roosevelt Elementary School. The former principal at Roosevelt was not a supporter of the superintendent. In October, the superintendent moved the incumbent principal to a central office desk job with little responsibility. The superintendent informed Carmela that the move of the incumbent principal was only partially political. There were other motives. The school was a hotbed for teacher unrest, test scores were low, parents were uninvolved, and school board attention was diverted to grievances that seemed to be streaming from Roosevelt. The irony of this situation was that the former principal maintained a strong core of supporters. The principal had passed favors around, maintained little teacher discipline, and had literally run the school as a country club for favored teachers. The superintendent did not paint a rosy picture for Carmela. Carmela recognized the challenges, but was assured of the superintendent's support and decided to accept the position.

The superintendent told Carmela that he wanted her to address the faculty before they left for the summer. She was not sure of the political climate in the school. As she prepared to address the faculty, she realized that there would be no central office staff to introduce her. It was to be Carmela's show. The superintendent told her that he did not want the faculty to perceive her as his puppet. Carmela felt her level of anxiety rise. She thought of what she had learned in college. She thought of her mentor. She wanted to call her mentor, but an inner feeling told her it was time to leave the nest, it was time to fly.

POLITICAL COMMUNICATION

Carmela McKenzie's communication and political skills will receive a severe testing. She will be quickly assessed by each member of her staff. They will make judgments based on their initial impressions. Future meetings with Carmela will be used by the staff to *bolster* their original opinions. First impressions count a great deal. Carmela does not have time to do a needs assessment. She does not have time to meet individually with the faculty. She does not have time to set up small focus groups with parents within her school community. These are excellent actions if there is preparation time. Carmela does not have this luxury. Carmela has to rely on her communication and political skills to be successful.

REFLECTION

Recall the first impression you had of your current supervisor. Was it positive or negative? What were your feelings?

Our research in many schools in different parts of the country regarding organizational dynamics indicates a clear pattern. In nearly every school (or every organization for that matter), there is a small group of people who work hard to make sure the organization succeeds. Carmela can count on these people as natural supporters. On the other hand, there is an equal percentage of people at the other end of the spectrum whom Carmela will never please. They will work to subvert everything she attempts. They will resist change in any form. They want to run the school and have Carmela act as their puppet. Each of these groups represents approximately 16% of the school population. The vast majority of the faculty, 68%, who are under the "bell curve," are not sure of the direction they should take. Should they accept Carmela and support her? Or should they resist Carmela and work to undermine her efforts? Unknown, because the action is covertly carried out, the outcome of this silent battle for the hearts of the majority faculty will determine Carmela's success. Carmela's political job is to move this 68% toward those who cooperate with her. If she can move the 68% toward her supporters she will isolate those who try to obstruct her. Their political games will be exposed as the rest of the school chooses to move forward with or without their cooperation. In essence, Carmela needs to focus her attention on the group of people who will determine her level of success.

As Carmela contemplates her first meeting with the faculty, she needs to consider her political message and the manner in which she will communicate this political message to her faculty.

TIP

Do not waste your time with those who will obstruct your every move.

THE POLITICAL MESSAGE

The political message describes Carmela's style of operation. Make no mistake—Carmela's political message is sent to the faculty by the end of the meeting. Some messages bolster the original message, while others flagrantly oppose the political message to which the staff has grown accustomed. Carmela's *political message* will provide answers for her staff to these questions:

♦ How will Carmela operate?
♦ Will Carmela share power?
♦ Is Carmela rigid or flexible?
♦ Can Carmela be trusted not to hurt me?
♦ Can Carmela be trusted to support me?
♦ Will Carmela be fair?
♦ What kind of leadership will Carmela provide?

Carmela's staff seeks the answers to these questions. A negative answer to one question will often close the minds of the staff to Carmela's response to the remaining questions. We believe that people want to work for an effective supervisor—a supervisor who is fair, just, and operates with the best interests of the group in mind. It is Carmela's responsibility to demonstrate that she is fair, just, and has the staff's best interests in mind.

The first issue, *how does the supervisor intend to operate*, provides Carmela with an opportunity to demonstrate that her intention is to be fair, that she seeks to collaborate and not act arbitrarily. Obviously, these are the right words to say to any group; however, they will become the standard by which Carmela is judged. One of the authors recalls when a new principal invoked words of openness, trust, and fairness at his first meeting. The new principal then secluded himself in his office. There was no perceived attempt to collaborate. There was no perceived attempt to listen. This was not the principal's intention. His actions communicated a message much different from his words. He did not understand that words have to be backed up by actions.

Carmela can prevent this mistake. She needs to *frame* her intentions within the organization's *context*. When we speak of *framing*, we speak of how Carmela views her audience and how she approaches her communication task with this audience. For example, when Carmela looks at her audience at the first faculty meeting, will she view them as enemies out to destroy her career? Or will she view them as caring people who may be confused by the turn of events? Her choice will be critical to her success.

TIP

Frame situations positively. Look for the best in people and situations.

Framing is a key ingredient to Carmela's success. It is by framing that Carmela releases or locks in her long-established biases and stereotypes. By looking at people and situations optimistically, Carmela releases her personal biases and stereotypes and communicates a sense of well being to her staff. Carmela can make her staff believe that they are appreciated, trusted to do a good job, and competent. Framing in a positive manner is an affirmation of human dignity. Carmela should look for opportunities where problems exist. She should look for the good in people and generate a sense of confidence. At this point she is effectively communicating. This is not false optimism. It is a realistic optimism through which Carmela communicates that the world is a friendly place, the organization is a good place to work, and that the people who work here are good human beings. This is an important communication and political tool.

REFLECTION

How have your previous supervisors framed the people in your unit? The students in your school? Or the members of school board? Has it been optimistic?

In the *political* sense, we speak of relationships, formal and informal, that exist between and among the individuals in the organization. If we define *politics* as the art of getting things done in a democracy, then we have to understand how things are accomplished in the organization. Carmela has to be a political realist. She cannot ignore the political context of her environment. Carmela has ideas of how she wants to accomplish her agenda, but if it does not fit into the political context, she will constantly be embroiled in a struggle.

When we speak of context, we speak of the *political, socioeconomic, intellectual,* and *aspirational* features of the context. If Carmela is not aware of the different characteristics of context, then Carmela is likely to develop a distorted frame of reference. These four areas are interrelated. In terms of the *political context*, it is important for Carmela to understand how her staff relates to each other, if they have been used to *dominating* or *collaborative* leadership, and their level of involvement in decision making. The answers to these questions inform Carmela as to the degree to which she may successfully alter the context. Carmela must recognize and influence the context.

As Carmela understands the context, she develops a *political map* of the organization. The *political map* indicates the formal ways business is conducted in the organization. For example, Carmela may not care for the supporters of the previous principal, yet a member of that group may be a key *political player* in generating support for Carmela's initiatives. The identification of these players is an important political consideration.

REFLECTION

What would a political map of your organization look like? Would you be able to identify all of the key political players?

When we speak of the *socioeconomic context,* we want to understand the cultural context of the community. There is a difference in the understanding of the application and use of power in higher and lower socioeconomic environments. In higher socioeconomic environments, the members of the community, in general, have a college education and expect to be involved in the process. This attitude is conveyed to the school board, the superintendent, principals, and teachers. Students expect to have their opinions heard and are encouraged to participate in the school governance process. This is in strong contrast to what happens in lower socioeconomic communities, where people have a different view of authority. In this type of community, Carmela is a powerful person who provides benefits or punishment. There is an expectation that she will use power. When power is not used where it is expected, Carmela is considered weak. There are other socioeconomic contexts. We use these extremes to indicate to Carmela that she has to be aware of the community expectations of the use power.

Carmela has to consider the *intellectual context.* The *intellectual context* refers both to the community and school. Within the community there may be schools with separate intellectual contexts. One school may consider itself "college prep," while another school may consider itself the "football school." In terms of the intellectual context, Carmela must realize that the more intellectual the context, the greater the demand for process and information. On the other hand, the less the intellectual context, the greater the emphasis that may be placed on emotions and intuition. In the former case, Carmela will be expected to have a substantive understanding of the issues that surround her role. If she brings any initiatives to her staff, she is expected to have data to support her arguments. If Carmela fails to do her homework, she is politically naive. This does not mean that Carmela, in a "less intellectual" environment, is able to get by with substandard work. It means that Carmela must approach the issue from a different perspective. The homework needed to be done by Carmela requires rigor and the additional component of considering the emotional aspects of the issue.

Carmela has to consider the *aspirational context* of the community and of the organization. In some organizations, the *aspirational context* is extremely high where there is an expectation of success. There is an expectation that the students will succeed. There is an expectation that everything the school does is done well. Conversely, there are organizations where the members just expect to survive. They operate on a daily basis. They move slowly, if at all. Carmela, in the former case, can move her staff at high speed. She is seen as a poor leader if she moves too slowly. In the latter case, she is seen as a poor leader if she tries to move the group too quickly. In each of the these four organizational contexts, we believe that Carmela must recognize the context and work politically to create an effective structure for change.

The second issue refers to Carmela's *willingness to share* power. This provides Carmela with an opportunity to demonstrate to her staff that power is used in the best interests of the school community. A positive environment is created when Carmela uses power for the benefit of her staff. When power is shared, it is beneficial. As the flow of power emerges, many members of the organization question if Carmela is a power sharer or a power hoarder. In the latter case, Carmela controls and hordes power as a means of dominating her organization and its people. Supervisors who hoard power are inherently insecure and have little faith in either others or themselves. On the other hand, supervisors who share power understand that they are not so much sharing power as they are turning it loose in a controlled fashion so that those who want to use power have access to its potential to benefit themselves and their organization. This framework is one of trust. This type of supervisor believes that subordinates use their power in an interdependent context. It is a trust in self, because Carmela is able to let go of the need to guard the *reserves* of power.

REFLECTION

What have been your experiences of supervisors sharing power? Have they willingly shared power? Have they limited the amount of power they are willing to share?

When Carmela lets go of the need to hold onto power and allows the staff access to power, she becomes a skilled political operative. Her people are empowered, allowed to learn from their mistakes, and encouraged to discover ways to further the political interests of the organization. Carmela McKenzie's most effective approach is to model this behavior in her interactions with the members of her staff. People learn more effectively from the examples she sets rather than from the words she speaks.

The staff will consider whether Carmela is *rigid* or *flexible*. This provides Carmela with an opportunity to demonstrate her leadership style. She communicates her style with every decision that she makes. Each time Carmela communicates a decision to her faculty, students, parents, or community she demonstrates flexibility or rigidity. We believe that Carmela must discover a *balance*. If Carmela is continuously flexible, she is viewed as anchorless. The staff believes they have no central focus. This creates a sense of insecurity, especially during turbulent times. There are times when Carmela needs to be rigid.

For example, let's suppose that some faculty members approach Carmela McKenzie and inform her of instructional plans which are inherently detrimental to students. When Carmela analyzes these plans, she recognizes that they are poorly conceived. When Carmela questions these plans, the staff members inform her that this is the way they operate and do not intend to change. Carmela has no choice but to be rigid in holding the faculty members to higher standards which meet the criteria inherent in good educational practice.

TIP

Do not blink when you know you are right!

Carmela does not dictate the practice for the staff to follow, she challenges the staff to meet a higher standard. In this sense, she is flexible. In the sense that she does not bend from good educational practices, she is rigid. A balance—Carmela knows when to be flexible or rigid. A simple heuristic that Carmela can follow in this regard is: *"If it does not violate our value system, I can be flexible. If it challenges our value system, I must be rigid."*

The staff wants to know if Carmela *can be trusted not to harm them.* Carmela needs to build trust to gain political support. Some supervisors naively believe that if they act politically, they have political support. By acting politically, they assume that they can *charm* people to their side. Charm has an effect, but its effect is short-lived. People look for substance. When the members of the organization are looking for substance, they are really looking for *trust.* Trust is a simple concept in the Carmela–staff dyad. It means that Carmela acts with the staff's best interests in mind. The majority of her staff members want to see the organization succeed, to see the supervisor succeed, and to personally succeed.

Employees want to see the organization succeed when their identities are associated with the organization. Carmela is a political supervisor when she works to forge links between her staff's identity and the organization's identity. One of the most effective ways of accomplishing this task is to increase the level of staff participation in the organization. This participation must be linked to reward. Carmela can use *appreciation, reward,* and *recognition* as political and communication tools. *Appreciation* means that Carmela communicates a sense of gratitude to the employee for his or her choice to work in the organization. It provides the employee with a sense of meaning and a sense that his or her contribution is understood. *Appreciation* is a deceptively powerful tool for Carmela. To use this tool effectively, Carmela needs to know each employee. She cannot appreciate a staff member if she does not know him or her.

Reward is an important political and communication tool in linking the employee's identity with the organization. Many employees are turned off by words. They want to see action. Reward has to be something tangible. Employees must feel they are receiving a benefit. The benefits that employees receive fall into three categories: financial reward, perquisites, and status.

REFLECTION

How are appreciation, recognition, and reward applied in your work unit?

In educational organizations, most supervisors are not able to provide financial rewards to their employees. This requires Carmela to use *perquisites* and *status* rewards as means of assisting the identification process. *Perquisites* may include attendance at conferences, parking privileges, and so forth. Carmela can be creative in the development and distribution of *perquisites*.

When Carmela does not make a clear connection between the *perquisite* and the employee's action she is accused of playing favorites. However, when the connection is clear, employees recognize Carmela is working in their best interests and demonstrating the organization's gratitude for the employee's contribution.

The third way for Carmela to create associative links between the employee and the organization is through *recognition*. It is an important human need to be recognized. Most people are seldom recognized in a public sense for their contribution. *Recognition* needs to be substantive. Many efforts at recognition are poorly conceived and give the appearance of being contrived. There has to be substance attached to the recognition. The person receiving the recognition needs to know why they are being recognized. They need to know that Carmela understands the reasons behind the recognition.

TIP

Make perquisites a public happening. This is a good way of shaping employee behavior.

Here is an actual example of the poor use of perquisites. The school principal brought a bag to a teacher and asked her to place her hand in the bag. The teacher pulled out a candy bar with the saying "Thanks for the good job" printed on the wrapper. The teacher thought the principal was referring to her recent work on an instructional committee. She was disillusioned when she learned that nearly every teacher received the same candy bar! When recognition is done in a public forum, those in attendance need to know the reasons so they can take pride in the recognition of one of their own. They need to know to develop an ownership in the accomplishments of each other and in the accomplishments of the organization.

Employees contribute to Carmela's success when they realize Carmela acts in their best interests and is a decent and competent human being. However, the staff members' view of competence can quickly change to incompetence if Carmela places her personal success above that of the organization and its employees. Personal success is often associated with ambition and a desire for power. If Carmela acts selfishly, she will not engender strong political support even though she has organizational political leverage.

EMPLOYEES WANT TO SEE DECENT HUMAN BEINGS SUCCEED

A decent human being is one who is kind, considerate, and compassionate. It is a person who likes other people, likes to be near other people, has a sincere smile, and understands the problems that are associated with being human. On the other hand, there are arrogant, mean-spirited individuals who do not give us a chance to like them. They communicate a sense of domination instead of kindness. They are comfortable when they are in control. The problem that these people have is that when they fall, there is no one to hold a net for them. There is no one to warn them when they are about to step in a hole. The employees wait to see them fail. This is not the case for the decent human being. People bend over backwards to help them succeed. They work with and for them. They want to belong to the same team as the decent supervisor.

Being decent is not sufficient. Carmela has to be competent. In the end, employees recognize that Carmela's competence is important to their well-being. The organization cannot survive an incompetent human being. It can survive a less than decent human being. It is better when both are working together. When we speak of competence, we mean that Carmela has a set of "benchmark" skills. Lombard and McCauley suggest a series of benchmark skills (Fig. 8.1).[1]

---

[1] M. Lombard and C. McCauley, "The Dynamics of Management." *Technical Report #34.* Greenville, NC: Center for Creative Leadership (July, 1988).

FIGURE 8.1. BENCHMARK SKILLS

- ◆ Awareness
- ◆ Compassion
- ◆ Composure
- ◆ Decisiveness
- ◆ Flexibility
- ◆ Interpersonal relationships
- ◆ Knowledge
- ◆ Preserving
- ◆ Problem solving
- ◆ Resourcefulness
- ◆ Selection
- ◆ Supervising
- ◆ Team player
- ◆ Warmth

These benchmark political and communication skills are competencies that are mandatory for today's supervisor. When mastered, Carmela has a sense of competence that is personally felt, projected, and received by others. Talking cannot compensate for competence. Competence is the root of personal power and personal power is the root of political power. People like to be associated with competent people. They know that competent people, if they are ethical, operate in their best interests.

Awareness is Carmela's ability to perceive her strengths and weaknesses. When she is able to honestly assess her ability, she is more open to the help of others because she realizes that she does not have all the pieces to the puzzle. *Compassion* is Carmela's ability to counsel, empathize, and communicate a sense of connection at the heart level with employees. *Composure* is Carmela's ability to be "cool" in stressful situations. Employees need to be able to anchor themselves to a rock during times of turbulence. If Carmela is not composed, then panic is likely to set in among employees. *Decisiveness* is Carmela's ability to make a decision and to act. She is able to stop the flow of information and recognize, even with limited information, where action is needed. She displays confidence, so she is able to act and, through her actions, communicate to the employees that the organization is not paralyzed. *Flexibility* is Carmela's ability to bend when it is essential. Carmela understands the differences between being tough and compassionate with employees. She can move between extremes according to the situation. Flexible supervisors "read" situations and apply the appropriate remedy. *Interpersonal relationships* involve Carmela's ability to cooperate with the members of her unit and with others outside of her unit. It is also her ability to negotiate and mediate through differences that block progress. These interpersonal skills are often considered by many to be crucial since most of the problems that she faces are interpersonal.

Knowledge is Carmela's ability to learn quickly the different competencies associated with her job. Carmela is not expected to have detailed knowledge of everyone's job, but she needs to have knowledge of where the unit fits into the organization. This "big picture" knowledge serves as the source for developing a correct vision. *Perseverance* is Carmela's ability to endure in times of difficulty. It is Carmela's ability to remain enthusiastic and resourceful. It is Carmela who communicates, through her actions, that she is not about to quit, and it is Carmela who inspires employees to remain steadfast. This kind of action enables the unit to overcome seemingly insurmountable odds. *Problem solving* is Carmela's ability to identify the symptoms, causes, and sources of problems. It means that Carmela has the ability and desire to address the root source of problems. *Resourcefulness* is Carmela's ability to move in ways that respond best to the present context. For example, Carmela needs to be resourceful in her meeting with the faculty. She is likely to be challenged. Carmela may be able to deflect challenges with humor rather than bitter attack. This would be a highly resourceful act. *Selection* is Carmela's ability to seek and hire competent people. In a sense, Carmela is a talent scout. Generally, the most effective way that supervisors change their organization is through the people they hire. If Carmela hires competent people, then it is likely that her school will be viewed as highly competent.

Supervising is Carmela's ability to delegate essential tasks, set motivating standards, and exhibit fairness in all dealings. In a sense, it is Carmela's ability to ensure that the work gets done and people are recognized for their efforts. *Team player* is Carmela's ability to work collaboratively with others in a team situation. When Carmela is a team player, other members of the organization identify more closely with her and with the organization. *Warmth* is Carmela's ability to generate a sense of approachability to the members of the organization. The members of the organization like to be around Carmela and to invite Carmela to their lunch table. Warmth means genuine "high fives," laughter, and crying. It is the humanness of Carmela being brought to the surface.

REFLECTION

How do you assess your benchmark skills? What are your strengths? What are your deficiencies?

EMPLOYEES WANT TO SUCCEED

Carmela's success depends solely on the success of her faculty and staff. She cannot do it alone. She cannot force her staff to succeed. To some extent she can pressure her staff. However, if she chooses to divorce her success from that of her employees, she will figuratively draw a line in the sand—she stands on one side and her employees stand on the other. A struggle will ensue. It is as if there are two groups at work within the work unit. One group is Carmela and a small band of supporters who are trying to change the organization. Another group, much larger, is passive at best, and actively resistant at worst. Carmela, in these situations, frequently is focused on public relations issues—the production of projects that give the appearance that the unit is productive. However, there is very little substance to these projects. As soon as Carmela leaves, the projects disappear and life is back to normal. The better question for Carmela to ask is, *"How do I make my employees successful?"*

We believe that this is a highly political question because more than anything that Carmela does, it generates a ground-swell of support for Carmela. There are few people in the American culture who do not want to be successful. Once people are taught how to be successful, their desire for continued success builds upon itself and serves as both motivator and reward. We suggest these guidelines to make employees successful for Carmela: *start small, provide feedback (public and private), increase the risks, stay with–stand back, and oasis converging.*

START SMALL

Each of Carmela's staff members is at a different stage of development and readiness for success. For some of her staff members it may be latent. For others, it is alive and burning. Carmela recognizes each employee's readiness for success. However, success is not brought about without the risk of failure; otherwise, the attainment of the goal has little meaning. The meaning of success rests in the fact that deeply buried in the human psyche is the need to achieve, to surmount obstacles, or to climb mountains. The employees have to be aware of the risks and of the rewards coming from the attempt at success. When Carmela starts small, the odds are increased that the project is successful. With small starts, Carmela guides the process, and coaches the participants to learn the tactics and strategies of success. The key point for Carmela is that the employees quietly become self. By starting small, Carmela gradually increases the risk and the concurrent reward associated with the success. Before long, Carmela and her employees are tackling large projects with zeal and confidence.

PROVIDE FEEDBACK—PUBLIC AND PRIVATE

Carmela needs to communicate with her staff members. Her staff members need to know if they are on the right path, have taken a wrong turn, or have stopped too long to gaze at the scenery. In providing feedback, Carmela is called on to be *cheerleader, counselor, motivator, advisor,* and *evaluator.* We consider the act of communication a highly political act in that the human psyche is fragile. When Carmela criticizes a staff member who believes he or she is competent, it is as if Carmela had taken a knife and plunged it deep within her staff member's heart. It is nearly impossible for the staff member to get past the words to listen to her criticism.

REFLECTION

Think of how easily you are discouraged or angered if someone you trust criticizes your work.

As *cheerleader,* Carmela McKenzie must be filled with enthusiasm and not consider the public possibility of failure. The sun is always shining. The sky is blue. Rains fall only when needed. There is an energy. Everyone is a star. Everyone is recognized. Someone must bring this type of energy to the organization. It has to be Carmela. If Carmela does not believe this to be the case, then Carmela demonstrates a lack of confidence in the members of the unit and their ability to achieve the goal that has been set.

As *counselor,* Carmela McKenzie moves from the public world of the cheerleader to the private world of the employee. In this world, Carmela seeks to discover the motivations, fears, and desires of her staff members. She guides her staff members through a process where they see their participation is in their best interests. As any competent counselor understands, this process is slow and is most effective when the counselor serves as a sounding board as staff members unravel their confusion. This takes time and is an investment in the employee. This is an investment in Carmela's career. This is an investment in the organization.

As *motivator*, Carmela McKenzie fluctuates between the public and the private worlds of the staff member. Feedback given to the group brings a connected sense to the faculty. It is an announcement of how they are doing together and how far they have to go. The feedback that Carmela provides in a private sense is pointedly addressed to the individual needs of the staff member. For example, Joe Rameriz, the science teacher, is not motivated by investing time in a collaborative project. However, Joe wants to get his doctorate at the local university. Carmela recognizes Joe's needs and helps Joe see the connections between participation in the project and doctoral studies. Once Joe makes this connection there is no stopping him, because Carmela helped Joe to discover a key to his motivation.

As *advisor*, Carmela reaches into her storehouse of knowledge to assist the faculty as they move more and more deeply into their project. Here she acts as guide, suggesting and educating, never preaching, always present to provide the faculty with essential advice. The advisor suggests, never tells. The advisor is soft-spoken, never loud. The advisor lets the faculty discover what was always present.

As *evaluator*, Carmela challenges her faculty. She clearly communicates the standards the faculty needs to meet to be successful. She charts their progress toward standards that are *fair*, *just*, and *honest*. To do less is an insult to the intellectual integrity of the faculty. It would suggest that the goal is meaningless and was fabricated to manipulate the faculty. Evaluation occurs in a public and private fashion. It occurs in a public fashion when Carmela asks the group to evaluate their progress and their outcomes. It happens when she asks the group to answer the questions, "How did we succeed?" "How can we improve upon what we just completed?" In this way, she is challenging the group to look at their success and not to rest on their laurels. In a private fashion, she constantly evaluates the work of each staff member. Most times this is accomplished informally over coffee or in casual meetings. At other times, it is formal. The private evaluation is most successful and meaningful when conducted in informal sessions where "evaluation" is not the operative term.

REFLECTION

How does evaluation occur in your unit. Does it serve to motivate or discourage?

Each of these roles helps Carmela to provide feedback to keep members *focused*. It is through feedback that staff members are connected to one another. It is through feedback that staff members eventually realize success. Carmela views feedback as a continual learning mechanism where she and the group constantly appraise each other.

INCREASE THE RISKS

Carmela accentuates the growth of her faculty by *increasing the risks*. When the risks are increased, so are the chances for intrinsic or extrinsic reward. The faculty has to understand the increase in risks. Yet, they must see this as the only alternative to their course of action. One of the problems that supervisors face in social organizations such as schools is that they are publicly funded and that the employees see little or no need to take risks unless there is a legislative threat to alter the organization's traditional way of operating. We suggest that Carmela not wait for the external motivation. When the faculty understands that they are part of some great movement, they want to be part of that movement. As Carmela increases the risks, the faculty is not fearful. They assume that this is their normal pattern of behavior.

We see this in operation every day in schools. In some low-performing schools, new principals are brought in to dramatically turn the school around. These principals have grand schemes. They set arbitrarily high standards and they fail. They never realize that when a person is learning to high jump, the bar is set at a height which the jumper can barely clear.

Then the bar is moved an inch, not a foot. If it were moved a foot, the psychological challenge would overwhelm the body's physical ability. Eventually, the high jumper is clearing heights which only weeks before would not have been attempted. It is this same process that Carmela must use with the members of her organization. Increase the risks, but increase them in gradients of 2.8%.

REFLECTION

Recall a time when your work unit was challenged, where the risks were high. How did your unit pull together? What was the feeling of your group when you succeeded or failed?

STAY WITH–STAND BACK

Here Carmela McKenzie demonstrates perseverance with the task. She cannot let go. She cannot become excited about another project and let this present project hang. It is her energy that sustains the project. It is her energy that feeds the members as they work through to conclusion. It is her energy that continually serves as a motivation for the employees as they move forward. Many supervisors make a critical judgment of leaving the task just when success can be seen at the edge of the horizon. When they leave, the group recognizes that the importance of the task is no longer a central focus. It is lost. Once it is lost, recovery is nearly impossible. When we speak of *staying with,* we are speaking of the essential leadership trait of completion. Carmela can and should move authority for the project toward staff members. In this way, when the project is completed, the highest compliment that can be paid to Carmela is that "we never needed you." It is here that Carmela *stands back* and allows the staff to take the credit. Carmela must suppress her desire to shine in favor of praise being harvested by staff members. This is solidarity at its best.

OASIS CONVERGING

There is a time for members of the group to celebrate. There is a time for reaping the rewards. There is a time for resting. There is a time for recuperation. Carmela must recognize these basic human motivational needs. It is here that Carmela allows her staff members to visit the oasis. It is in the oasis that her staff regains its strength. It is in the oasis that her staff creates the myths that surround its journey. It is in the oasis that her staff creates an oral history of the journey. When oasis time is neglected, her staff members psychologically and physically break down. They are not able to replenish the storehouse of energy they need to continue on the journey, especially if the risks are increased. Carmela needs to understand the amount of time that is needed for recuperation. If Carmela allows her staff to remain too long in the oasis, they begin to settle. Carmela needs to rekindle the desire to explore and motivate the group to push onward toward new goals.

Carmela needs to link these factors. The effective supervisor realizes these three pieces are interdependent. Therefore, Carmela needs to ask, "How do I let the faculty know that I want them to succeed?" As Carmela answers this question she will notice the faculty deepen their trust in her.

FACULTY CONCERNS ABOUT GAINING SUPPORT

The fifth issue that Carmela must face is *the faculty's concern over whether or not they can gain her support.* Carmela cannot support the faculty until she is fully cognizant of their underlying needs. This requires both political and communication skills. It requires political skills since leadership is impossible without followership. Her staff will not follow her if she is unable or unwilling to translate their needs into action. In a sense, Carmela is the expression of the staff's needs. A supervisor with political skills is able to sense the *needs* and *aspirations* of the members of his or her organization.

The *needs* of the members are related to their expressed concerns. These needs are concerned with the present moment.

They are the member's immediate concern with survival, safety, personal gain, and environment. If Carmela is able to discern these immediate needs and acts on them, she will win politically. These needs create a common bond between Carmela and her staff.

Discerning the needs of the staff requires communication skills. Carmela needs to listen. There are different listening posts that need Carmela's attention if she is to discover the needs her staff. These listening posts include her staff members, the population that her staff serves, district leaders, people not part but aware of her school's function, and the environment.

TIP

You're in it together or you're in it alone.

MEMBERS OF THE UNIT

This is the primary listening post. These are the people who have to be heard. The manner in which they are heard is highly political. It is political because Carmela operates in a democracy. Therefore, her staff members have a right to be heard. Carmela has a duty to hear them. How they are heard is also political. They need to be heard in an open and safe environment, one in which information is shared. We believe that private meetings are a part of this process. If Carmela has a relatively small staff, personal meetings are easily made part of the schedule. If Carmela has a large staff, personal meetings may be time-consuming and counterproductive. Carmela needs to be concerned with giving everyone an opportunity to participate. How does Carmela McKenzie accomplish this task? In our book, *Hands-on Leadership Tools for Principals*, we demonstrate how faculty meetings are organized to facilitate healthy and productive discussion on single issues.[2] These same principles apply to all meetings. As a guideline, Carmela needs to have meetings that are focused, safe, and organized.

REFLECTION

How well are the needs of your work unit heard by your supervisor? Is there an ongoing attempt to encourage members of your work unit to express their needs in a safe, inviting environment?

Much of what Carmela hears from the faculty is colored by personal interests based on biases, filtered information, and stereotypes. This is true of most people as well as organizations. We constantly see reality in a narrow sense. If the faculty are able to see the reality of their work environment objectively, then Carmela's search for information is completed. However, the reality for Carmela is that the search for information has just begun. The members of the unit are able to provide an important political piece of information. They need to internalize that they are heard. How does Carmela let the members of the unit understand that they are being heard? Primarily by asking questions to make sure that she understands what is being said. Use questions to understand the motivation behind the comment. For example, if we were in attendance at Carmela McKenzie's faculty meetings we might overhear this dialogue:

Teacher A: The parents in this community just do not care. That's our major problem. They just do not care.

Carmela: I do not understand what you mean by "They just do not care." Can you give me some examples?

---

[2] R.L. Calabrese, S.J. Zepeda, and G. Short, *Hands-on Leadership Tools for Principals.* Larchmont, NY: Eye On Education (1996).

Teacher A: Sure. There are plenty of examples. Look at our Back-to-School Nights. They are poorly attended. It's always the same old people who attend these things.

Carmela: Parent attendance at our Back-to-School Nights is poor? Are there other areas where you would like to have more parent participation?

Teacher A: We need a parent's advisory board that represents all of the parents. If they felt they had a voice in the school, they would want to be part of the school.

Carmela: From your comments, I understand that parents would probably participate in greater numbers if they felt included in the school and that their voice was being heard.

Teacher A: Exactly. That is my whole point. We need to incorporate parents into our school. We should have representatives at this meeting.

Carmela: Thank you. That is so helpful.

Carmela's careful application of questioning elicited a clearer response from the teacher. The teacher who initially criticized parents really wants greater inclusion of parents in the school. If Carmela had prematurely ended the conversation, she would not have discovered the teacher's hidden concerns. If Carmela stopped at the first comment, the teacher would have left the meeting knowing that he or she had expressed him- or herself, but not believing he or she was heard.

THE POPULATION THAT THE UNIT SERVES

This essential listening post provides a different perspective for Carmela. It is listening for impressions. This is a political skill because it is the beginning of the building of alliances between Carmela's unit and other units. When Carmela speaks with the principals in the district and listens to their perspectives, she is validating their experience. She is also laying the groundwork for collaboration between her faculty and the faculties of other schools. Failure to recognize this listening post is a common error. Carmela cannot afford to operate under the myth that her unit is an independent entity. Units within an organization operate interdependently. When they operate interdependently, the larger organization is more effective.

The information that Carmela receives is based on *hearsay, competition-driven biases,* and *environmental distance.* Carmela filters out fact from fiction. Carmela is careful. She has no way of knowing the principal's motivation. America is a competition driven culture. It is part of who we are as a people. That sense of competition is often taken to extremes, and people manipulate situations to further personal advantage. Carmela needs to be aware of the possible competitive motives of the principals in her district. If these motives exist, she has to carefully screen the information that is given to her.

TIP

Be on guard as to the accuracy of the information you gain through hearsay.

ENVIRONMENTAL DISTANCE

Environmental distance refers to the physical and emotional distance of the units. A grade school is further distanced from a high school than is a middle school. A school on one side of town is further distanced from a school on the other side of town than a school within walking distance. Distance fragments messages. Most information gathered in this environment is of the *bolstering type. Bolstering* information supports the work of the speaker. It supports his or her unit and informs the listener that the speaker's unit has a place of primacy.

THE LEADERS OF THE MACRO ORGANIZATION

This is a critical listening post for Carmela. Carmela needs to translate the messages she receives. Carmela must take primary responsibility for the correct interpretation of these messages. This may seem unreasonable and unfair. We agree on both accounts. However, we consider the taking of responsibility of the communication translation to be of critical political importance. In the end, it is Carmela who is criticized for not understanding. Carmela's subordinates are not asked to shoulder responsibility, nor will Carmela's superordinate.

REFLECTION

How frequently do you take responsibility for understanding the messages you receive from subordinates as well as superordinates?

Carmela receives communications from a superordinate in two ways: directly and indirectly. When the superordinate sends messages in *direct communication* there is no equivocation as to the intent of their meaning. As supervisor, Carmela is given a direct charge as to what is to be accomplished. One of the authors, upon being hired as a high school principal, recalls being brought into the superintendent's office to meet with the superintendent and the school board president. The school board president looked at the newly hired principal and said, "Your job is to straighten this school out. I mean we want the poor discipline cleaned up. Do you understand what I am saying to you?" There was no equivocation in his words. He was straight and to the point. The principal understood the charge. This exchange is rare.

Direct communication seldom occurs. As a result, Carmela must seek to discover the hidden meaning behind the superordinate's words. For example, let's assume that the following conversation occurs between Carmela McKenzie and her superintendent:

Superintendent: Carmela, I hired you to clean up the mess at that school. I believe that you can do it.

Carmela: Can you be more specific? What exactly do you see as the problem?

Superintendent: You'll find out soon enough. Your faculty will challenge you from day one. It won't be an easy job.

Carmela: The faculty is a problem?

Superintendent: I'm tired of getting grievances. It takes my time. It takes the board's time. The previous principal did not know how to work with people.

Carmela: Were teachers the only group that caused my predecessor problems?

Superintendent: No! The parents were always calling board members because the principal wouldn't listen to them. Then the board members complained to me.

We can see from this conversation between Carmela and her superintendent that the superintendent's directive to "straighten out the school" may really mean, "I do not want to be involved with hearing complaints about your school. It is your task to handle issues at your level." On one hand, Carmela could have interpreted the superintendent's instructions literally and created insurmountable problems for herself and her school. On the other hand, her attempt to discover what the superintendent really meant provides her with a clearer direction.

When translating the intent of a superordinate's messages, we suggest that Carmela consider the following heuristics:

- The superordinate is primarily concerned with his or her personal advancement and survival.
- The superordinate clearly does not want to be involved in micromanaging.
- The superordinate wants your group to be successful so that the superordinate will receive praise for hiring you and for the success of your group.

♦ The superordinate is telling you only what they think you should hear; more often than not, you are not hearing the full story.

These are political heuristics. The superordinate may clearly articulate whether they have the best interests of the school in mind. However, it is our belief that when superordinates feel a threat to their personal security, they make decisions in their own self-interests. There are exceptions. There are superordinates who make decisions based on a moral stand or other-centered value structure. These people are rare. We hope you are one of these rare exceptions.

Indirect communication refers to the memorandums, side conversations with other political operators, and the behaviors of Carmela's superordinate. Carmela received a memorandum from the superintendent addressed to all principals. The memorandum suggested that principals read the teacher's contract prior to the start of the new school year. The superintendent is telling the principals that the contract is to be followed and that the principals need to be aware of its contents. The superintendent may also be telling principals that grievances based on the teacher's belief that the contract was violated should not occur.

At times, the superordinate sends messengers to subordinates. These messengers do not act with the authority of the superordinate; however, the power of the message is still the same. Carmela needs to understand this pattern of communication. The messenger is a carrier. The messenger carries messages to and from the superordinate. Carmela uses the carrier to communicate with the superordinate. Carmela has to discern the forms of indirect communication that exist in her district. She may disagree with the culturally established way of communicating; however, her success depends more on how she adapts to the normative means of communication.

One other form of *indirect communication* that Carmela must identify is the superordinate's indirect forms of political communication. These forms include *invitations, proximity, and referencing.* When these forms are present, it is a sign that the superordinate approves of Carmela's work. This is a signal of a good evaluation. When these forms are absent, it sends a strong message that the superordinate is distancing him- or herself from Carmela.

REFLECTION

What are the formal and informal means of communication in your work unit? How have you used indirect means of communication to send messages to superordinates?

Invitations are events that the superordinate asks Carmela to attend. If they are with the superordinate, they are of special significance. It means that the superordinate wants to be identified with Carmela. Those with most-favored status receive significantly more quality invitations than those who do not have the same status. *Proximity* infers that the superordinate wants to be seen with Carmela. She may be asked to sit next to the superordinate. This is *proximity*. Carmela gives herself *proximity* by choosing where she sits. However, her choice is meaningless. When *proximity* is offered by the superordinate, it is a sign that superordinate wants to hear her ideas and be associated with her. *Referencing* refers to the superordinate's use of Carmela's name in meetings or in memoranda. This is the superordinate's way of communicating to others that he or she needs to look at Carmela's work. It bolsters Carmela by informing others that the superordinate is pleased with her work. *Referencing, invitation,* and *proximity* provide important indirect communication clues which are critical to Carmela.

PEOPLE NOT PART OF THE UNIT BUT AWARE
OF THE UNIT'S FUNCTION

This is an important listening post for Carmela. All members of the organization have a deep interest in the function and well-being of all units. Complementary units work together to further mutual interests. They seldom, if ever, want to work together to serve another unit's interests to the total exclusion of their own. Similarly, there is a competitive instinct among similarly leveled units. These units are competing for the superordinate's attention. Units that achieve primacy have greater access to resources and approval of programs and in times of stress are protected.

THE ENVIRONMENT

The environment is the physical and psychological surroundings of Carmela's worksite. The physical environment communicates, in a positive sense, that this is an environment that is well cared for by the members. It is easy to spot a physical environment that does not send that message. It is drab at best. It disinvites others to be a part of its place. One of the authors took a class to visit an elementary school in a large urban setting. The elementary school was located on the edge of the urban environment. The group initially passed by the school, mistaking it for a juvenile detention facility. Literally, the school was surrounded by 8-foot-high fences and had no external windows. Yet, the school was not located in a "high crime area." The school had a physical presence that was disinviting.

The psychological environment is influenced by the physical environment. If the members are happy, cooperative, and see each other as important contributors, it is likely that the psychological environment is inviting. On the other hand, if there is constant warfare or backbiting among members, if cliques dominate and Carmela has favorites, a negative psychological environment exists. This is one of the key issues that Carmela has to defuse as she leads her school.

> **REFLECTION**
>
> Describe the physical and environmental messages sent by your worksite.

CONCERN ABOUT FAIRNESS

The sixth issue is *the concern of the members of the organization regarding fairness of Carmela.* Employees realize that the *easy* supervisor is poor at best and a disaster at worst. This does not stop employees from testing Carmela's resolve. This testing determines the limits that Carmela sets. Once the limits are set, the employee's major concern is whether Carmela adheres to the same limits for all members. Fairness, in the eyes of the employees, relates directly to how they perceive their treatment in relationship to the treatment afforded other members. It is a personal judgment. Carmela ensures fairness by treating all staff members equally. She brings a sense of compassion by not abusing her authority and by consistently applying the same standards when distributing rewards.

> **REFLECTION**
>
> Have you ever been in an organization where people were not treated fairly? How did the unfair treatment impact the organization?

WHAT KIND OF LEADERSHIP IS BEING PROVIDED?

The seventh issue concerns the leadership Carmela is providing the members of the organization. Carmela is locked into a world which demands strong managerial skills and requires strong leadership. This type of leadership is action-oriented, close to the members of the organization, sensitive to the welfare of the members of the organization, hands-on, and aggressive in protecting the organization's interests. This type of leadership provides the political and communication skills that are highly regarded in successful supervisors. These are skills to be used in the best interests of the organization and the members of Carmela's immediate unit. The degree to which Carmela is able to craft these skills into an art is directly proportional to the success of her unit.

PULLING IT TOGETHER

FIELD BASED PROJECTS

1. Identify four supervisors. Ask the members of their units to recall their first impressions. How have these supervisors lived up to the first impressions that they gave? What were the political messages that these supervisors conveyed during that initial meeting, if any at all? Did they create problems for themselves and their units that have become insurmountable? Ask the members what they would have liked to have heard from their supervisors at that initial meeting.

2. Design a political map of your current organization. Identify the flow of power and positions (names) of people who have a locus of control. Can you identify political patterns on your map? Where are the entry points? Where are the dead ends? Where are the potential political pitfalls? Use this map to explain the political dynamics that occur within your organization.

3. Identify the socioeconomic context of your organization. Do the members of the work unit mirror the values of the surrounding community? How effectively do the members of your organization interpret the surrounding socioeconomic culture? What is the relationship of the members of your unit to the surrounding culture? Is it one of superiority? Is it condescending? Is it one of submission? How does the interaction between the surrounding socioeconomic culture and your unit affect you unit's efficiency?

FIELD BASED ANALYSIS

1. Collect all available written communication between your work unit and the larger organization. What forms of political considerations are communicated in this manner? Are you able to discern where the political influence exists in the larger organization through the written communication?

2. Conduct a focus group with teachers and administrators related to the forms of political communication in your school district. Use the focus group to determine the political position of your unit in comparison to similar units, locations of allies and opponents. Ask the focus group for recommendations related to improving the strategic position of your unit. What are the pitfalls in the strategies that have been suggested?

3. Collect all available data related to your unit's appreciation, reward, and recognition of its members. Is there a systematic process to appreciate, reward, and recognize members? What is the reaction of members to any existing process? What forms of appreciation, rewards, or recognition would be motivational to members?

IF YOU WERE CARMELA MCKENZIE...

How would you react to the superintendent's request?

How would you respond to a lack of superordinate support at your first faculty meeting?

What kinds of political messages would you want to convey to the faculty?

How would you relate to the previous principal?

How would you frame your view of the faculty?

How would you use your relationship to your previous principal to support your current assignment?

Would you be willing to share power with those who still support the previous principal?

How would you assess your benchmark skills?

How would you work with a faculty member who is politically powerful but not a team player?

How would you would work with an assistant principal who is not supportive but is politically connected to members of the school board?

What would be your primary method for developing political support within your unit?

RESOURCES

BOOKS

Hamton, J., ed., *AMA Management Handbook*. New York: AMA-CON (1994).

Sergiovanni, T. & Starratt, R., *Supervision: A Redefinition*. New York: McGraw Hill (1992).

Spendolini, M., *The Benchmarking Book*. New York: AMACON (1992).

WEB SITE

http://www.nassp.org/ (Home page for the National Association of Secondary School Principals).

INDEX